TO GEORGE ROWLEY, WHO KNEW THE POWER OF THE BRUSH

MARK TOBEY

BY WILLIAM C. SEITZ
THE MUSEUM OF MODERN
ART, NEW YORK

IN COLLABORATION WITH
THE CLEVELAND MUSEUM OF ART AND
THE ART INSTITUTE OF CHICAGO

Distributed by Doubleday & Co., Inc., Garden City, N.Y.

Published by The Museum of Modern Art, 1962
11 West 53 Street, New York, N.Y.
All rights reserved
Library of Congress Catalogue Card No. 62-18507
Designed by Susan Draper
Printed in Germany by Brüder Hartmann, West Berlin

CONTENTS

ACKNOWLEDGMENTS

Much of the material on which this book is based was drawn from a series of conversations with Mark Tobey during the spring of 1962. I should like to thank him for the patience and candor with which he considered the many questions I raised, and Marian Willard for her gracious cooperation.

It is a pleasure to convey my appreciation, and that of the Trustees of The Museum of Modern Art, The Cleveland Museum of Art, and The Art Institute of Chicago, to those who have given help in preparing the book and the exhibition that led to its publication; and to the collectors, museums, and dealers whose assistance made this exhibition possible. For assistance in gathering documentary material I am grateful to Katharine Kuh, Devorah Sherman, Arthur L. Dahl, Colonel and Mrs. A. H. Hooker, Jr., and Charles Seliger. For assistance in arranging the exhibition: Richard E. Fuller, Edward B. Thomas and William J. Lahr, of the Seattle Art Museum; François Mathey of the Musée des Arts Décoratifs, Paris; Ann Forsdyke and Bryan Robertson of The Whitechapel Art Gallery, London; Elmira Bier of the Phillips Collection, Washington; Lucy Mitton of the Willard Gallery, New York; Otto D. Seligman of the Otto Seligman Gallery, Seattle; Ernst Beyeler of the Galerie Beyeler, Basel. For photographic assistance: Marvin P. Lazarus, George Uchida. For special assistance: Mr. Tobey, Miss Willard, Mr. and Mrs. Arthur L. Dahl, and N. Richard Miller.

I also wish to thank those who worked on the book: Helen M. Franc, who edited the text; Monroe Wheeler, James Thrall Soby, and Alicia Legg, who read and criticized it; Irma Seitz; Lucy Lippard and Miss Legg for the appendices; Inga Forslund, who prepared the bibliography; Sally Kuhn and Constance Clodfelter, for typing and transcription of taped material; and Susan Draper for her fresh book design.

WILLIAM C. SEITZ, *Associate Curator*
Department of Painting and Sculpture Exhibitions

Mark Tobey, 1962. Photograph by the author

FOREWORD

James Abott McNeill Whistler was the first modern American painter to leave a lasting mark on European art. He was awarded an international prize at the Biennale of Venice in 1895, and in 1905, two years after his death, he was given a large retrospective exhibition at the Ecole Nationale Supérieure des Beaux-Arts in Paris. Mark Tobey, a Midwesterner who sixty years ago lived the life of Tom Sawyer along the Mississippi, is the only other American to have achieved these marks of international renown. After his retrospective exhibition at the Musée des Arts Décoratifs in 1961 an English critic wrote that "Tobey is considered by the prominent painters of the School of Paris, as well as by established European art dealers, to be the foremost living American artist." A critic of France – that country which in the past has occasionally been less than hospitable to the art of outsiders – wrote that "Tobey is perhaps the most important painter of our epoch." He is regarded as both the most European of our painters and one of the most American; in the genetics of ideas his art is seen as a link between present and past, East and West. Yet Tobey's avant-garde style was arrived at in all but total independence of continental modernism, and it precedes the advent of the New York School, with which it is often – and not incorrectly – associated.

At present, it would appear, Tobey is even more highly regarded abroad than he is at home. It behooves us, therefore, to study his painting and thought with a new seriousness; not only for this reason, or because he paints pictures that are profound, masterful, and delightful to behold, but also because his unique development throws valuable light on our culture and its relation to that of Europe and the Orient. As a purely autonomous phenomenon, moreover, the slow growth and sudden crystallization of Tobey's art is a thing of beauty, an affirmation of human sensibility and commitment.   W. C. S.

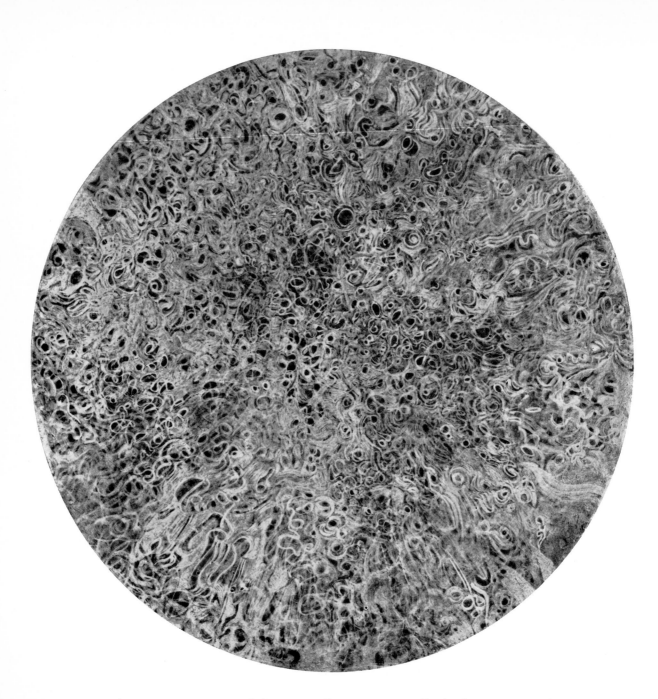

8 *World.* (1959). Tempera, 11³/₄″ diameter. Collection Marian Willard Johnson, New York

TOBEY'S WORLD VIEW

The earth has been round for some time now, but not in man's relations to man nor in the understanding of the arts of each as a part of that roundness. As usual we have occupied ourselves too much with the outer, the objective, at the expense of the inner world wherein the true roundness lies.[1]

I remember when I saw a water spider and it brought down a bubble of air and placed it over its nest – a magical and fantastic thing. — *Mark Tobey*

Mark Tobey's paintings are seldom large, and many are smaller than this page. They are usually rendered in tempera or watercolor rather than oil, in unassertive colors. His surfaces are worked with brush strokes that can be explosively bold, but are more often as delicate as the strands of a spider web or as ephemeral as smoke rising from a cigarette. At first some of his works seem two-dimensional, but if one is willing to look long enough, the eye and mind are led to enter a unique world of form, space, and meaning. One discovers, sometimes quite unexpectedly, that the smallest and least arresting work can become vast in depth, extent, and significance. The difference between the actual size and potential scale of Tobey's pictures can be startling. Recalled in memory, if one knows them well, they combine and expand to define a spherical universe of forms and ideas.

Before anything else, a work of art should command attention as an energized object. The ideas that engendered it must have been fused with their medium to form a new substance. For this reason it is often wrongly demanded that a painting decant its entire meaning at a glance. Tobey's world of ideas must be entered through his paintings, but they can be fully understood only through familiarity with the experiences and convictions that surround them. For this reason his thought will be studied here before the forms, and even the subjects of the paintings. This sequence will exemplify the thinking behind Tobey's brush, and demonstrate the interpenetration of his art and life.

The artist, as Tobey realizes, is not a cool-headed intellectual: "What supremely rational person," he asks, "can keep from going to sleep?"[2] With amusement – but not wholly in jest – he notes that journalists have called him a "Northwest mystic," and "the sage of Seattle." Although current thought craves extrarational experience, it distrusts living saints, mystics, or prophets; and Tobey has never claimed such a status. Nonetheless, to deal with his views accurately one must recognize that they are often mystical and religious. Like Kandinsky, Klee, and Mondrian, Tobey sees the highest reality as spiritual rather than physical. His world view – properly so called because it is more embracing than the metaphysics of the three European painters – is theological as well as aesthetic. Tobey readily acknowledges the debt his art owes to his religion. Although he painted before his conversion to the Bahá'í World Faith in 1918, the existing content of his art is a direct outcome of this revelation.[3] The premises of Bahá'í doctrine which support and permeate his thinking can be reduced to three interrelated concepts: unity, "progressive revelation," and humanity.

"The Oneness of Mankind is like a pivot around which all the teachings of Bahá'u'lláh [the founder of Bahá'í] revolve."[4] Bahá'í temples must have nine sides, not only because nine, as the largest integer, "symbolizes comprehensiveness, oneness, and unity,"[5] but because followers of each of nine great world religions can enter through separate portals, meeting with the other faiths in common worship at the central point. Bahá'í teaching is often couched in celestial imagery. Its Godhead is depicted as radiant and spherical, like the sun. Ultimate reality is indivisible, and does not admit of multiplicity. A botanical metaphor is used to reconcile Bahá'í "oneness" with the stubborn part-whole problem: humanity is likened to a tree of which each individual is a part, and the product of a single seed. Bahá'í humanism, inseparable from the premise of unity, opposes all social divisions and barriers which can engender hostility, injustice, or strife, whether personal, national, or religious; and it advocates an auxiliary international language, international mediation, world peace, and the ultimate unification of peoples in a single world state. The priority of this social doctrine is plain in the assertion of 'Abdu'l-Bahá (third in the line of Bahá'í spokesmen) that if a religion "rouses hatred or strife . . . absence of religion is preferable" and "an irreligious man better than one who professes it."[6]

Bahá'í provided Tobey with aesthetic as well as social and religious principles. He has often stated that there can be no break between nature, art, science, religion, and personal life. The belief in an ultimate unity – visualized as a central focus or enclosing sphere, conceived as a common underlying substance as in early Greek monism or modern physics, known through an irrefutable experience as in mystical religion, or derived from a universal principle as in Buddhism – underlies a great body of human speculation. Few religions, however, have given the concept of *oneness* such pointed emphasis, and few modern artists have dealt with it as explicitly as has Tobey. Its most dramatic impact on his world view lies in the Bahá'í reversal of Kipling's dogma, "East is East, and West is West, and never the twain shall meet," by the conviction that "all humanity whether it be in the East or in the West may be connected through the bond of this divine affection; for we are all the waves of one

Conflict of the Satanic and Celestial Egos. (c. 1918). Watercolor, 18¹/₂ × 12″. Owned by the artist

The Void Devouring the Gadget Era. 1942. Tempera, $21^{1}/_{2} \times 29^{3}/_{8}''$. Owned by the artist

The New Day. (1945?). Tempera, $12^3/4 \times 23^1/4''$. Collection Mr. and Mrs. Arthur L. Dahl, Pebble Beach, California

sea."[7] "The East and West will embrace as long-lost lovers," Tobey predicts, quoting Bahá'u'lláh.

As a "universal" religion, Bahá'í recognizes a progression of prophets, martyrs, saints, and teachers of various faiths, culminating with Bahá'u'lláh but including Abraham, Moses, Zoroaster, Buddha, Christ, and Mohammed. Each is held to be the bearer of a common truth cast in the form that served the needs of a particular time and situation. As 'Abdu'l-Bahá emphasized when he lectured in the United States in 1912, the radical concept of "progressive revelation" carries with it an identification with advanced opinion and knowledge in all fields of thought: "Religion is the outer expression of the divine reality. Therefore it must be living, vitalized, moving and progressive. If it be without motion and non-progressive it

is without divine life; it is dead. . . . All things are subject to divine re-formation. This is a century of life and renewal. Sciences and arts, industry and invention have been reformed. Law and ethics have been reconstituted, reorganized. The world of thought has been regenerated. Sciences of former ages and philosophies of the past are useless today. Present exigencies demand new methods of solution; world problems are without precedent. Old ideas and modes of thought are fast becoming obsolete . . . for this is clearly the century of a new life, the century of the revelation of the reality and therefore the greatest of all centuries."[8]

'Abdu'l-Bahá cites the progress of "this radiant century" – "the century of motion, divine stimulus and accomplishment" – "the century of light" – as evidence that "the new day" is at hand: "The East and West can communicate instantly. A human being can soar in the skies or speed in submarine depths. The power of steam has linked the continents.... Day by day discoveries are increasing. What a wonderful century this is!"[9]

There is a terrible alternative, however. With amazing insight for the period before World War I, 'Abdu'l-Bahá cites the destructiveness of modern armaments, and warns that "if we remain fettered and restricted by human inventions and dogmas, day by day the world of mankind will be degraded, day by day warfare and strife will increase and satanic forces converge toward the destruction of the human race."[10] Tobey's very early *Conflict of the Satanic and Celestial Egos* (page 10), painted shortly after his introduction to Bahá'í and influenced by Michelangelo and William Blake, depicts this struggle,

as, in contemporary terms, does *The Void Devouring the Gadget Era* (page 11).

Except for the eschatological warning, the parallel between 'Abdu'l-Bahá's progressivism and early avant-garde writings such as Apollinaire's *The Cubist Painters* is striking. Even before Tobey's belated familiarity with advanced modern art, Bahá'í doctrine propelled him toward innovation, and surely lies behind the following statements: "At a time when experimentation expresses itself in all forms of life, search becomes the only valid expression of the spirit...."[11] "I am accused often of too much experimentation, but what else should I do when all other factors of man are in the same condition? I thrust forward into space as science and the rest do. The gods of the past are as dead today as they were when Christianity overcame the pagan world. The time is simi-

The Retreat of the Friend. (1947). Tempera, 10 × 14³/₄″. Collection Nathaniel Saltonstall, Boston

lar, only the arena is the whole world."[12]

Tobey has sometimes been loosely regarded as an apostle of Zen. The error is apparent in comparing the "oneness" of Zen with that of Bahá'í. Zen is not a religion, nor is it a pantheism or mysticism in the Western sense. Inherently anti-intellectual and anti-theoretical, it can have no theology. Differentiation between God and nature, nature and man, reason and emotion it regards as absurd. Bahá'í, by contrast, is totally anthropocentric and Western, though it originated in Persia. Criticized from a Zen viewpoint, indeed, Bahá'í is dualistic, dividing reality into parts.[13] Not only does Bahá'í theory separate godlike man from nature: it distinguishes natural law, as a controlling force, from the creatures it is held to direct. Beings "lower" than human are "captives of nature,"[14] for the animal is unable to deviate from patterns of instinct and desire. Man, because he is endowed with intellect, reason, and spiritual powers, can probe the mysteries of nature, control natural law and even deviate from it. He is therefore not a part of nature but its ruler: "higher and nobler by reason of the ideal and heavenly force latent and manifest in him."[15]

As an artist, and because of his knowledge of Oriental art and Zen, Tobey finds a closer affinity of man to nature. Augmented from many other quarters, Bahá'í views on unity, humanity, and progressive revelation nevertheless operate in every phase of Tobey's painting after 1920, and he has painted many explicitly religious subjects. Inasmuch as Bahá'í upholds the innate truth of all religions, some paintings interpret Christian themes such as *The Last Supper, Homage to the Virgin* (page 69), *The Deposition* (page 68), and *The Flight into Egypt.* Though deeply concerned with their significance, Tobey transforms them as a composer might an earlier musical form, motif, or specific composition; upon or into the ancient subject he builds "a modern complex structure."[16] More general in theme, *Western Splendor* (1943, page 58), "a façade in grays and ambient light" is "a wall of memories of churchly splendor surviving the ages."[17]

Another group of religious paintings is specifically related to Bahá'í. Because he draws on a doctrine without an iconic tradition, Tobey is free to visualize the words of the Bahá'í spokesmen freely, and to originate his own pictorial conventions. Most important among this group, perhaps, are the works depicting martyrs, prophets, and the idea of progressive revelation. For Tobey, following Bahá'u'lláh, the "body" of the martyr is his teaching, and his death is symbolic. *The Cycle of the Prophet* deals with the rhythmic sequence of divine spokesmen; *Movement around the Martyr* celebrates the rebirth that follows his sacrifice as it takes form in social change, great music, art, and architecture; *The Retreat of the Friend* (page 13) concerns the quiet retirement of the saint and friend of mankind as he makes way for another; *The Gold of the Martyr* contrasts spiritual with material wealth; *The New Day* (page 12) designates the period when peace reigns, and "the sun of arts and crafts is manifest from the horizon of the heaven of the Occident."[18]

Tobey's religious paintings, like those of Rouault, are noteworthy not only because he is a truly contemporary artist, but because they arise from conviction rather than as commissioned church decorations. He is venerated by the Bahá'í movement as their only great artist, but when asked, after a lecture at one of their meetings, about an official "Bahá'í art," Tobey replied that modern literacy has made didactic art unnecessary, and that "art would be free in a Bahá'í world."[19]

Meyer Schapiro once observed that works of art are the "last handmade, personal objects" left in our industrialized world.[20] It could also be said that artists are among the few professionals whose lives, personalities, and beliefs are organically integrated. Tobey believes in inspiration and intuition. "Mankind today," he complains, quoting Bahá'u'lláh, "has lost the power of scent."[21] Tobey's likes and dislikes, ethics, religion, amusements, goings and comings, aesthetics—his very faults and weaknesses—make up one entity, whole and clearly defined even in its contradictions.

World-famous and no longer young, Tobey is as independent, volatile, and unpredictable as he must have been as a tyro fashion illustrator in his twenties. Now as then he is a romantic figure. No one, observing the white hair billowing back from his high forehead or the closely trimmed beard that shapes his chin, or catching a glimpse of him in the street wearing a rough tweed coat and a beret, could fail to realize that he is an artist. The image of Tobey wandering in the crowded streets of New York, Paris, Hong Kong, or Seattle, his senses alive to passers-by, buildings, weather, smells and sounds, pausing to observe them with curiosity, amusement, and annoyance replacing each other in his mind, is both accurate and symbolic. Movement – or, more specifically, *migration* – is a leitmotiv of Tobey's life and art. He is fascinated by the skid-row drifters that haunt the Pike Place Public Market in Seattle; in part, perhaps, because he also has been a migrant, as restless as one of the twisting or drifting brush signs that activate the space of his paintings. Tobey's quest, like that of Bahá'í, is for peace – for the freedom and tranquility to paint and meditate. He dislikes crowds; but who has painted them with more understanding? He is a bad traveler, nervous in automobiles, uncomfortable in trains, and ill at ease in airplanes; but who has painted man's wanderings so meaningfully? As a friend once remarked, Tobey seems to paint what he most professes to dislike.

Tobey is an amateur musician and composer who plays the piano to relax and clarify his visual imagination; he has written expressive prose and good poetry, and is an insatiable reader of novels, poetry, books on botany, biology and travel, mystery stories, or whatever is at hand. He loves the film, concerts, and the theater. His memory is boundless. Tobey's physical and spiritual migrations, therefore, have grown into an inexhaustible store of ideas and images, with facets widely separated in origin. The position of an initial impression in the whole is established slowly, as if maturation were essential for spirit and form to adjust to each other.

For an artist caught in the whirlpool of modern life a degree of egoism is essential for survival. Tobey knows that one cannot escape the limitation of the self – that "you are you whether walking backward or forward";[22]

but his art is directed outward: "Oh, Tobey, he's always interested in nature, but I'm interested in myself," a painter-friend complained. Tobey sees the ego, in its selfishness and separateness, as a limitation to be transcended: "'The era of adolescence is over.'[23] We must concentrate outside ourselves. As we arrive at maturity we must take on new responsibilities. We all feel a separateness – we wish that a drop of water would soften our ego."[24]

Tobey's thinking organizes itself through a series of contradictions or, perhaps better, oppositions. He admires modern science, but feels we are blinded by its achievements, and he is suspicious of psychology and psychoanalysis, because they have led us to obsession with psychic pressures: "Focused almost completely on this, we forget that there are today great men in the religious field with as much to offer."[25] He believes our society overvalues comfort, money, and possessions, with a result that is mechanizing and dehumanizing: "We worship the young. We want *so* much muscle power for *so* much money." He sees a strange belief in the "immortality of the body.... We're in the age of denial of everything but physical existence. The thing we've got to fight for is humanism – it's the highest thing we know; we can't mechanize ourselves out of existence."[26] When drawn together, Tobey's scattered criticisms of modern life constitute an admonition depicting a society which, like that of Rome in the fourth century, is at a crossroad: one direction is toward fulfillment and the other toward extinction. When the question was raised, during a symposium in 1949, whether anyone in ancient Rome knew their culture was in decline, Tobey commented: "I presume there were some, but they were called Christians."[27] It is in this light that *Imperator* (page 16), which depicts a cracking Constantinian head, should be interpreted.

In the struggle between the spiritual and the material the United States, and especially New York, is a major battlefield. Very recently a French interviewer, discerning two currents, one active and the other contemplative, in Tobey's art, drew from him the following comment on his paintings of cities: "No doubt I did them because I am an

American painter. I cannot be indifferent to the swarming crowds, multitudes, neon signs, movie theaters, to the noises that I hate of modern cities."[28] Tobey painted *Broadway* (opposite) amid the misty groves of Devonshire: "Of course when I did *Broadway* I did it because I loved it, because I had experienced it. It was in my bones, but I could paint it best when I was farthest from it." In New York, as elsewhere in America, however, Tobey sees the color, individuality, camaraderie, fantasy, and tradition that pleased him disappearing. Double-decked buses on Fifth Avenue are gone, and fine old buildings are being callously demolished: "These city planners and these boxers have killed all that. There isn't any roof line any more." The new glass buildings rising overnight from gutted sites are for Tobey not an inter-national style—they are "international death." Though he has been drawn toward America's human vitality, its picturesque folkways, and some of its landscape, Tobey has never been entirely at home here. On leaving an exhibition in Chicago which included Pollock and Rothko (whose painting he especially admires), his sharpest memory was of a work by Edward Hopper, whose factual poetry translated to him "the loneliness and solitude that is in American psychology, and that thing talked more to me than all those other paintings.... I have lived all over America except the South;... actually lived these damned streets on Sunday where not even a cat is seen.... It's that kind of a life that can live without extensions. Isolationism. But not isolated by continents and water—isolated from spiritual currents...."

Among tensions in Tobey's thought other than that between the material and spiritual is the opposition of past to future. The two directions resemble each other: "To rediscover the past is to move forward. There is no surcease when we constantly destroy what we have built. The future is carved with the implements we created before it was upon us. The past offers the art student different roads, all converging towards his present. Today's present appears different, more confusing; voices cry from all quarters. It used to be dangerous to know. Today it's dangerous not to know. What was close and established must now make room for newcomers. There is much groaning and some growls. Art, forever free, seeks freedom from man's tyranny."[29]

Tobey's "philosophy" of art (if the use of the term can be permitted for an organic, rather than a systematized body of ideas) reflects his attitudes toward the past, present, and future, and also toward nontemporality. His experience had prepared him to respond with sympathy when, late in the forties, André Malraux hypnotized the reading world by dramatizing modern knowledge of art and its wide dissemination through museums, photographs and prints, art books, and technical advances. Tobey's art history began with the idealized figure painting and sculpture of the Renaissance—the style against which modern-

Imperator. 1944. Tempera, 16³/₈ × 12¹/₄".
Collection Mr. and Mrs. C. A. Crosser, Seattle

Broadway. (1935?). Tempera, $26 \times 19^{1}/_{4}''$.
The Metropolitan Museum of Art.
Arthur H. Hearn Fund, 1942

ism was in revolt, but which Tobey has never totally discarded. Gradually his horizon expanded to include the leading masters of Eastern as well as Western art.[30] To wander through a museum with Tobey is to share in a succession of responses, warm acceptances, and instant dismissals. In principle, he does not avoid influence from any quarter: "There is no such thing as a distinctly original artist. Every artist has his patron saints whether or not he is willing to acknowledge them. When an influence is strong enough, give in to it."[31] But Tobey's painting seldom shows specific derivation. Pervading though it is, the influence of China and Japan is general, and thoroughly assimilated. His "cubism" (see pages 45-47) was his own from the beginning. Some of the religious paintings intentionally reflect medieval stained glass, architecture, or Italian and Byzantine frescoes and icons. Totem poles and other Northwest Indian artifacts are both a subject matter and a plastic influence. A collector of all sorts of primitive art, Tobey draws no line between a gallery of art and an ethnological museum.

Some of his most recognizable derivations are from Near Eastern, medieval, and Oriental calligraphy and ornament, and from those primitive styles having graphic signs compatible with twentieth-century form. A list of such instances, some confined to a single work, would include Egyptian pictographs, cuneiform, Coptic and Peruvian textiles, Australian bark painting, Arabic, Persian, and Hebrew script, and Celtic illumination. This list could be augmented with another from the contemporary environment of billboards, street signs, scientific symbols, punctuation and other graphic devices, unexpected effects in picture-magazine photographs, the end papers of old books, and an endless inventory of markings, patterns, and structures in nature. More revealing, perhaps, than to ferret out the scattered sources of Tobey's graphic language is to indicate the ideology that explains its diversity: "When I was a young man, I never heard of Byzantine art. . . . Now, above the horizon has come the beauty of Byzantine art – not only that, but the art the colored people have, and the art of the Coptics, and all of the Orient and everything that has flooded the world.

"Now it seems to me that we are in a universalizing period. . . . If we are to have world peace, we should have an understanding of all the idioms of beauty because the members of humanity who have created these idioms of beauty are going to be a part of us. And I would say that we are in a period when we are discovering and becoming acquainted with these idioms for the first time. . . ."[32]

Tobey is moved by both constancy and change, and also by the nontemporalization – one could almost say "spatialization" – of styles: a "universal marshland, wherein lie forms of ancient ideas and cultures apparently unrelated to us but only waiting for time to reveal themselves upon the arc of our consciousness."[33] He sees Gothic art, for example, exhausting itself "in an electric light fixture in a café in the Far West."[34]

The many oppositions of Tobey's thought – religion and science, Orient and Occident, spiritual and material, evolution and timelessness among them – bring about the same equilibrium that he seeks in his painting: "It is a state of equilibrium which must be maintained if man is to move, to go forward."[35]

FORM AND PROCESS

No painters in history have tried to signify as much content with as little form as have those of this century, and few modern artists have assembled as rich a structure of ideas on which to draw as has Tobey. Considering how often he works with nonfigurative images, it is surprising how much of this content has been concentrated at the point of his brush. With such demands made on the medium, qualities sometimes thought to be secondary, such as gesture and tension, become at least as important as shape, color, or placement. In addition, with content so frequently connotive, allusive, and implicitly but not overtly evident, the process of seeing and understanding places special demands on the spectator.

The new linear and calligraphic image by which Tobey is known evolved in opposition to another vocabulary of modeled bulks, light and shade, and empty space. By now these traditional solutions have all but vanished from his work; yet, like a memory, their previous existence continues to be recalled. In attending to Tobey's "new" means, therefore, the "old" should not be forgotten.

LINE, PLANE, AND STRUCTURE

Threading Light: White lines movement symbolize light as a unifying idea which flows through compartmented units of life, bringing a dynamic to men's minds ever expanding their energies toward a larger relativity.[36]

In a pure state, line is without variation in tone, width, sharpness, or "attack." Usually (as anyone who has used a ballpoint pen or watched a jet cross the sky on a clear day should know) a line records a movement of a certain speed, regularity, and direction. Conceived as movement, line was the origin and is unquestionably the primary means of Tobey's painting, but because the brush is his favorite tool, lines are seldom without some variation. Line functions most effectively without color; indeed, unless a colorist is as skillful as Klee, Dufy, or Pollock in combining the two means, they are incompatible. Tobey avoids color when it would interfere with linear clarity. A characteristic of his linear structures so original and evident that it can easily be overlooked should be pointed out. His line, unlike that of most draughtsmen and painters, is most often (as in a photographic negative) light or whitish in tone, and set against a dark background.

Many of Tobey's works after 1935, as he has indicated, are entirely generated by line—that is to say by thin brush strokes with minimum variation. The linear method is announced in a pastel of 1933, *Cirque d'Hiver* (page 21). Though differing in degree of multiplicity, *Lines of the City* and *New York* (pages 64, 65) employ no other means. The multiplication of lines creates structure, and in these pictures symbolic architecture. In *Gothic* (page 58) each vertical suggests a shaft or pier, and each curve a vault or groin: one recalls that Tobey once worked in a drafting room, and that his elder brother was a structural designer.

Drift of Summer (page 57) and other nature subjects of 1942 use straight lines, bows, loops, or ellipses to make

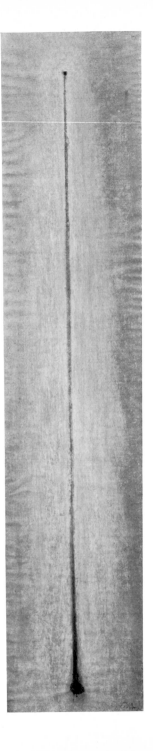

Space Line. 1953. Tempera, 26⁵/₈ × 5⁷/₈″. Willard Gallery, New York

exquisite references to the structures and movements of plants and grasses, insects, birds, and fish. The illuminated light path of *Threading Light* flows from compartment to compartment, pausing to delineate figures or other objects (page 55). In *Space Line* (1953, at left) a single ascending trace beginning at a point animates an iridescent void. The son of one of Tobey's students, who was in uniform, looked at a picture of this type for a long time and finally said: "I'm a pilot. When I get to the top of this, I'm in my plane."[37] *Space Line* actually originated from studies of the hollyhocks in Tobey's garden.

In realizing the possibilities of line Tobey goes further than Feininger, and even (if that is possible) Klee.[38] Hans Hofmann, whose painting and theory stress large color planes, criticizes linear painting because "we can lose ourselves in a multitude of lines."[39] It is precisely this attribute of linear multiplicity that Tobey was the first to utilize fully. He has made mazes, nets, masses, and universes of line, molded sculpture of lines, and constructed linear containers for modeled figures and objects. Thickened until they stand in space like rods, lines become dancing figures, piers, or the bars of an entanglement (page 63). He has made line the symbol of spiritual illumination, human communication and migration, natural form and process, and movement between levels of consciousness.

Planes, in Tobey's painting, usually originate in line. Moving line was an aspect of his "personal discovery of cubism" in 1922 (see pages 45–47). In *Northwest Still Life* (opposite) the swinging trace generates forms independent of the ghost-objects it surrounds. By this means Tobey not only developed movement but, as lines intersected, shapes and planes. In such pictures as *New York*, which are multiples of straight lines, it is as if one were looking through thousands of transparent walls, floors, and windows fading from view in a city-space cut into an infinitude of tiny compartments. In pictures of many other types, moreover, planes are a secondary means; in *Above the Earth* (1953, page 75), for example, an almost invisible geometric construction of lines is bare-

Cirque d'Hiver. (1933). Pastel, $16^7/8 \times 21^1/2''$. Collection Mr. and Mrs. Windsor Utley, Seattle

Northwest Still Life. 1941. Tempera, $20 \times 26''$. Seattle Art Museum. Eugene Fuller Memorial Collection

ly materialized by slight changes of tone; and even in such a work as *Omnia* (1952, page 24), which at first gives the impression of a worn and scratched surface, the scratches cross to suggest planes in ambiguous recession and, inevitably, space. The readjustments of lines, or tones between them, in Tobey's paintings can be so slight that the spectator is not always sure whether they originate in his mind or the artist's. Some of Tobey's greatest artistry lies at this threshold.

BRUSH

> *. . . Oriental fragments – characters which twist and turn drifting into Western zones forever speaking of the unity of man's spirit.*[40]

Although the distinction between *line* and *brush* is important to recognize, and easy to make in theory, it is not always clear in practice. If Tobey's most abstract paintings were arranged in a sequence from one category to the other, the steps would overlap. Needless to say many works would include both line and brush, and others would fall between the two. In other works, especially those including realistic images, line and brush are combined with more orthodox modeled and tonal passages. A few, even in the later period, would exclude both line and calligraphy. One can say, nevertheless, that when variations in width, tone, and edging become great enough, and when the continuity typical of line is broken, the threshold has been passed. And in their pure states line and brush are fundamentally different means: a sharp distinction, for example, exists between such a picture as *Voyage of the Saints* (1952, page 72) and the pictures on pages 66, 67, 74.

Tobey loves Titian and Rubens, worships Rembrandt and Cézanne, and regards Monet highly, yet his brush style owes little to Europe. He was bitten by "the handling bug" when he was barely twenty and hoped to become a magazine cover illustrator (see pages 43–44). And expressionist brushwork – that is to say the projection in pigment of personal anguish, joy, sexuality, or other overt emotion – is foreign to Tobey's temperament.

Detail of Tobey's line.
(from *City Radiance*, illustrated on page 64)

Detail of Tobey's brush.
(from *Tropicalism*, illustrated on page 66)

Attuned to the Oriental painters rather than to expressionism, he wishes to reflect the world outside himself, or express "higher" states of his own consciousness. But because his ideas are so powerful, and at base so Western, his brush almost never is imitative, Orientalizing, or overdecorative. Years of maturation preceded his East-West synthesis, and after it happened, in 1935, his knowledge of Oriental brush was immediately assimilated.

Tobey's description of certain of his strokes as "characters which twist and turn" is accurate and graphic. Often as three-dimensional as wood shavings, such strokes seem, like "light birds" bobbing on a shadowed wall, to be animated from within themselves – disembodied but personalized entities. This category of stroke, derived from Chinese and Japanese script but existing in a variety of forms, is typical of Tobey but by no means exclusively so. An inventory of Tobey's brush signs would include (to mention a very few types): acute or obtuse "V" forms and zig-zags which define rectilinear movements in space; random dots and particles; miniature plus-and-minus strokes like those once used by Mondrian; broad wave motions reminiscent of art nouveau; electrical tremors and vibrations; imperious gestures, as with a baton; odd shadows, blips, and ghosts of strokes; jabs with a spread or dry brush; fields of punctuation and code; vagrant, unmotivated touches that float on the air; and, in the magnificent ink paintings (sumis) of 1957, cataclysmic explosions of black energy in an electrified void.[41]

Tobey's signs, without specific reference to human or natural forms or to artifacts, still convey their activities and modes of existence. And, beyond the inherent expressiveness of any one stroke, its function and significance are determined by its context. One or many types can make a picture, and their divergence can range from the subtlest implication of variety within homogeneity to extreme contrasts of size, shape, and spirit. Individual brush strokes make up a grammar for which the total equilibrium of line, tone, brush, structure, arrangement, and figuration is the syntax.

SPACE, VOID, FLATNESS, AND "MASS"

My eye keeps focusing upon the opaque windows. Suddenly the vision is disturbed by the shape of a gull floating silently across the width of a window. Then space again.[42]

Tobey uses his surface as if it were a writing tablet. Taking as a norm one of the characteristic abstract works such as *Plane of Poverty* (1960, page 81), a Tobey could be superficially described as a panel entirely covered, up to its four corners, with a uniform network of lines or strokes. More truthfully stated, Tobey's surfaces are never uniformly covered; but even a varied painting such as *Omnia*, which Tobey refers to as "probably the most complex picture I ever made," can appear to an unprepared eye as a palimpsest covered with chance markings.

Untouched surface can also appear as unfilled and unlimited space – as a void. Of central importance for Oriental art, the idea of void in painting is new to Western art. Our tradition begins with the figure sculpture of the Greeks, who used the third dimension, as C. R. Morey wrote, "solely to define the independent existence of the subjects."[43] At the antipodes of Western humanism, Ch'an and Zen painting, and the spirit of which they were a product, look on the void as a creative force. Even when bulk is present, as in the T'ang period, it partakes of void. To the West total emptiness has the threatening tone of Tobey's frightening picture of 1942, so prophetic of the atomic disasters to come, *The Void Devouring the Gadget Era* (page 11). It is the Last Judgment in his warning against the dangers of materialism. A few small recent pictures, among them *Void II* (page 2), are films of color that coagulate into blackish shadow in the central area. But in general the void for Tobey is at one pole of a synthesis: he has sought to marry Oriental void to Occidental bulk.

Space to Tobey is more than visual, and it interests him more than surface. By the time his painting had developed beyond ordinary three-dimensional representation he found that he "really could touch space"; "it became a kind of living thing . . . like a sixth sense." In the outside environment, he realizes, humans are always dealing with space; cutting it up, eating and sleeping within it, enclosing it as architecture, or passing through it in travel: "Three-dimensional space consciousness is a real type of consciousness to me; but if you got in a fourth-dimensional space consciousness it would be something quite different, and then I don't think you would have the time sense between spaces." Modern air travel indeed has something of this psychological effect; the sense of space, as Tobey says, "collapses." He regards space as never empty: "Scientists say that . . . there is no such thing as empty space. It's all loaded with life." We know it to be teeming with electrical energy, potential sights and silent sounds, spores, seeds, "and God knows what all." The step from the physical to the metaphysical, between which Tobey insists there is "no break," can fill the void even with currents of thought.

If the entities placed in space by Tobey's brush remain separate they move actively or drift, but as their number is increased, void becomes occupied space, and finally matter becomes dominant. As it has been shown, the multiplication of straight lines at various angles generates the structure of architecture or, using other strokes and treatments, that of grasses, crystals, electrical fields, etc.

Covering the surface with less assertive lines, and filling the space more fully, results in what Tobey calls "mass." His usage does not denote a solid body of material but an aerated substance, bringing about "the dematerialization of form by space penetration." "I made lines into mass," he explains: "I want vibration in it so that's why it takes so long to build this up; because I want it to have air pockets. . . . Before I get to the actual painting I have to build up mass of line." This linear "mass" can also be seen as motion: "I cover my surface completely and I put my plastic elements into motion up to the four corners. Everything stirs, everything moves, everything becomes animated."[44]

It is not just space and depth that stimulate Tobey's imagination, but what goes on in them. A cult of space, he feels, is as boring as any other. He is always cognizant,

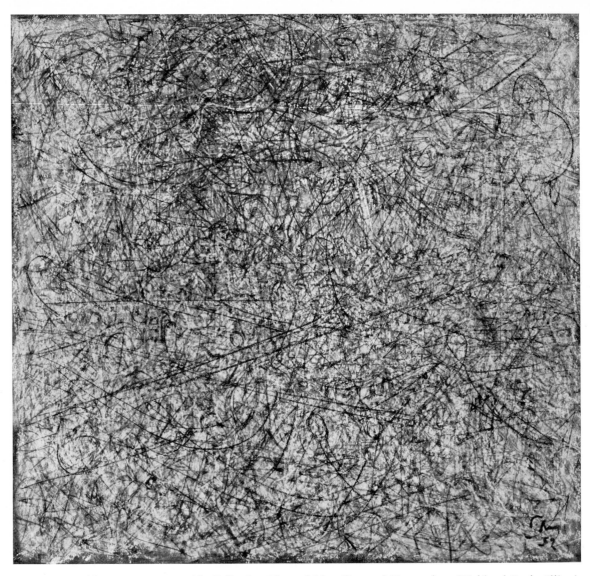

Omnia. 1952. Tempera, 28¹/₂ × 29¹/₂″. Collection Mr. and Mrs. Sigmund Kunstadter, Highland Park, Illinois

opposite: *New York Tablet.* 1946. Tempera, 24⁷/₈ × 19″.
Munson-Williams-Proctor Institute, Utica, New York. Edward W. Root Bequest

Broadway Boogie. 1942. Tempera,
$31^3/8 \times 24^3/8''$. Collection
Mr. and Mrs. Max Weinstein, Seattle

as *New York Tablet* (page 25) demonstrates, of surface, actual or illusory, as the complement of space, structure, or "mass." In this painting tracery is written on at least four planes that oscillate between separateness from each other and unification in a three-dimensional architectural image resembling the United Nations Secretariat (though the building was not finished until 1950, four years after the painting). At the rear of the composition stands a tablet surrounded by darkness. The frontal plane, emphasized by a line at its edge, is not parallel to the picture surface but tips into shallow depth. This plane does not appear warped, yet one cannot be positive whether it is the right or the left edge that recedes. The relationships are calculated to effect just such live ambiguity.

"MULTIPLE SPACE" AND "MOVING FOCUS"

Multiple space bounded by involved white lines symbolizes higher states of consciousness.[45]

Tobey and Pollock were among the first to paint "off the picture." By 1952, calligraphic homogeneity of surface had been called "apocalyptic wallpaper" by Harold Rosenberg.[46] Except in rare instances, Tobey has avoided this pitfall because his "white writing" was the outcome of two other related innovations: "multiple space" and "moving focus." They lie behind – and often within – the over-all calligraphic picture.

When Tobey was a young man, his friend Teng Kuei asked him why Western artists made pictures "that looked like holes in the wall." Tobey felt this to be a serious criticism. Linear perspective rivets the spectator to one spot, and freezes the objects represented into a single relationship, scale, and illumination system. Although *Broadway* (page 17) was the first painting to open form with a full brush, it is still controlled by one-point perspective and factual scale.[47] It is made up, Tobey says, of "some impressionism, some cubism, and writing." Partly because the subject is similar, centralized perspective shows like a ghost through *Broadway Boogie* (opposite), painted more than five years later. In the interim, however, Tobey had liberated his brush from perspective as

well as bulk – though even this break had been made, if not consolidated, by 1936. In *Welcome Hero* (page 60), painted immediately after *Broadway*, the empty space between buildings has been filled with "mass" and movement; walls are fragmented and – going beyond *Broadway* – the compartments of architecture, billboards, and other geometric details have broken away from the focus of the street. The outcome is plain in *Rummage* and *Threading Light* (page 54–55). Space becomes "multiple" by its division into compartments, but more than that, each cell has its autonomous size, position, and mode of visualization.

For the purposes of discussion, the looping white lines of *Threading Light* can represent (as in diagrams of eye movements) the new freedom of the spectator. True "moving focus," however, requires another step. In *Transition to Forms* and *Drift of Summer* (pages 56–57) of 1942, Tobey repeatedly readjusted his focus as he painted so that (as in a series of photographs printed over each other in different positions) hollows are filled, bulk is opened, and the surface is thus unified. Space becomes "compound" as the depth systems of the various foci interpenetrate, and the eyes of the spectator (reversing the Renaissance rule) are given no focal area or object (as in figure paintings or portraits) at which to rest. They are forced to move across the surface of the picture. "That type of painting in which you are not allowed to rest on anything: you're bounced off it or you have to keep moving with it."

COLOR

In Kyoto in 1934 Tobey saw "a great dragon painted in free brush style" on the ceiling of a temple. Its rhythmical power reminded him of Michelangelo. The spiritual intensity the Eastern and Western artists had in common is shared by Tobey's sumis, in which the name, and in a few instances (see pages 78–79) even the image of the dragon appears. The three painters also have in common their avoidance of color.

Although Tobey uses color beautifully and skillfully,

Universal Field. 1949. Tempera and pastel, 28 × 48¹/₈″. Whitney Museum of American Art, New York

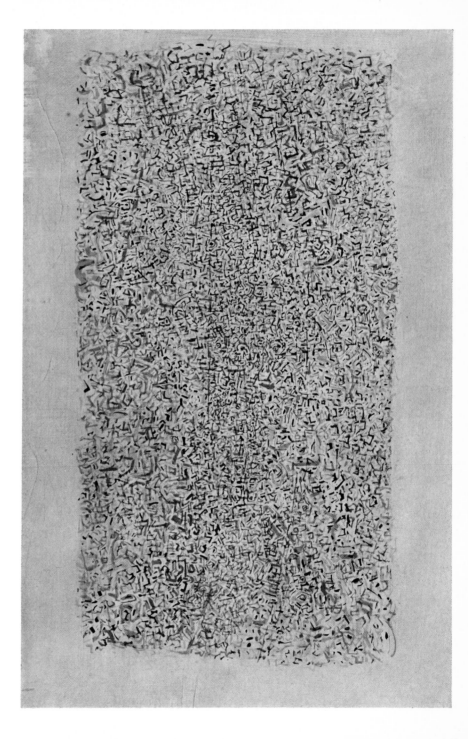

Universal City. (1951). Tempera, $34^3/_8 \times 24^7/_8''$.
Collection Marian Willard Johnson, New York

and in his youth painted on occasion with bright hues and rich pigment, color is the least essential of his means. He feels coloristic painting lacks profundity: "Color in the Orient is for children." Persian miniatures, fauvism, and the work of Matisse are "joy painting." Cézanne, though he was a colorist, was, like Tobey, interested in both sculptural and structural form. He was "too deep, too philosophical," Tobey feels, for unrestrained colorism. Hans Hofmann rejects the "impressionistic method,"[48] which disintegrates color planes, just as he does linear painting; but it is precisely this method and result that draws Tobey to Rembrandt, Turner, and Monet.

Tobey's central development was a struggle between sculptural bulk and its disintegration by space, movement, and structure. The problems that rose before him led him to turn away from color for tone and structure, as did Picasso, Braque, and Mondrian between 1910 and 1915: "Like the early cubists, I couldn't use much color at this point as the problems were complicated enough without this additional one."[49] Thus many of the finest pictures are virtually monochromatic. Nothing gives Tobey more satisfaction than to work within a narrow range of whites. He has remained a structural, calligraphic, and acutely sensitive tonal painter, but nevertheless has masterfully adapted color to his ends.

E Pluribus Unum (page 32) and the other pictures representing the colorful Seattle Market, and the paintings of Indian subjects, are painted in the ochres, earth reds, and grays of primitive Indian art. Many works of the forties and fifties employ a spectrum of iridescent tints, as does *Edge of August* (1953, page 39). Quite often Tobey uses an all-over tone of sepia, cream, gamboge, blue, or red to establish the mood of a work. He also uses colors adjacent to each other on the wheel, and with as much mastery as he does ranges of off-whites, beiges, tans, violets, warm and cool grays, or gradations within one color tone. In nearly every work of the "Meditative Series" (page 76, cat. nos. 79–83, 86), for example, he manipulates space and definition within a rigorously restrained palette of browns, violets, and earth reds. At low levels of intensity, he uses complementaries and other hue contrasts to intensify tonal form—touches of warm color against the smoky blue of *Universal Field* (page 28), oppositions of dull red and soft orange to cobalt in *Delta* (page 67), and a sparkling pointillism of muted hues in *Universal City*. Over the years Tobey's color has become increasingly higher in key: *Jeweled Jungle* (page 80) was painted in 1958, *Homage to Rameau* (page 52) in 1960.

EQUILIBRIUM AND COMPLETION

The "written" panel, by which Tobey is best known, lies at the heart of his style; but a variety of forms, various modes of representation, and a welter of ideas clamoring for expression make up its periphery. He is ready for "actual painting" by the time the surface is covered. The "mass" or structure at this stage is a malleable "marshland" that, by control and adjustment, can move toward more than one possible conclusion or connotation. The intensification of a geometric trace or two will bring to light a previously buried partition or compartment; by revising the tone or size of the "writing" within a defined area, its scale and depth can suddenly be made to shift in relationship to the adjoining area as if by a change of lens. Space can be folded back on itself as in *City Radiance* (page 64); "holes" can be opened through filled space to void, like patches of sky seen through clouds; a forward layer of strokes—stronger, larger, and sparser—can be added, transforming the original field into a teeming broth by which the bolder signs are nourished; representation can be added to abstraction, or an advanced manner can be directed backward toward earlier ideas.

It is such development, crucial for the outcome of Tobey's finest painting, that is least evident to eyes keyed to striking effects. It is at this point that the plastic sensibility of a spectator must meet that of the painter, whose final adjustments cannot always be separated from the visual reinterpretations of the spectator as his experience of the painting deepens. Often barely discernible but essential, certain of Tobey's earlier solutions or subjects—"layers of time"—recur. In the beautiful *Universal City* (page 29), for example, the irregularly shaped field of punctuation gravitates around a circumscribed dot that orders the whole abstract composition; and finally, to a spectator who has taken the time, the image of *Broadway* —the canyon of a crowded street, its buildings, and a movement-filled strip of sky—appears. In many works, usually vertical, a linear split, a shadow, or a tall tube of space or illumination in the central area controls the surface. *Written Over the Plains* (page 71) and *Universal Field* (page 28) gravitate around a focal nucleus.

As Gothic art is ascending, and as that of Mondrian gradually became spaceless and rectilinear, Tobey's form is globular. However rectangulated it may be, his structure extends in every direction—often there is no "up" or "down." His images usually end or fade near the frame, and vignetted compositions tend toward ovals. The bister-toned watercolors of 1950 fade inward and upward, curving into depth. Those works painted "off the picture," without concession to the frame, place one in the midst of an expanding universe, either microcosmic or macrocosmic. In the paintings "outside the earth," forms remain within the sphere of its attraction, and in certain of these (page 77), the agitated strokes are seen from across the curving segment of a sphere. Some of Tobey's apparently flat pictures, if looked at long enough, fall back above center in a domical or hemispherical vortex.

Although he values quietness, it is apparent that movement and process are central to Tobey's art. Few painters have originated more restless forms. The particles and movements in *Universal Field,* coming from all directions, can be seen as a visualization of the priority that modern science gives to energy over matter (though the picture was painted as a result of Tobey's first visit to an airport). Elsewhere forms swarm, merge, mass, divide—almost every verb of movement could apply to some passage. Painting for Tobey is more an analogy with life than it is a professional technique. Always evident, this conviction is especially to be noted in the Meditative Series. Visual prayers, these small, profound communions with God, nature, and the self transcribe the *activity,* as distinct from the subject matter, of meditation.

"We artists must learn to breathe more," Tobey wrote in 1951.[50] A static painting, however well done, has "no breath in it; it doesn't breathe." In approaching the completion of a work, Tobey always hopes to arrive at a point where he is no longer painting for himself—when his hand, like that of the Zen archer, moves without effort. The painting process must go on until all forces have converged on their objective, but must stop while the work still breathes: "If you don't know when to stop, and carry the picture too far, you have a corpse on your hands."[51] Here, static unification and finish are contrasted with the state of equilibrium which is Tobey's criterion for life and wholeness on any level of experience. It transfers the creative process from painter to spectator before its energy is frozen. This intent is implicit in his definition of a good *informel* painting which, he says, "is not supposed to strike or intrigue the eye of the spectator. . . . It is only slowly, habitually, little by little, that an *informel* painting attracts the interest of the viewer."[52] "It is better to feel a painting than to look at it," Tobey says, drawing an old Chinese principle from his memory.[53]

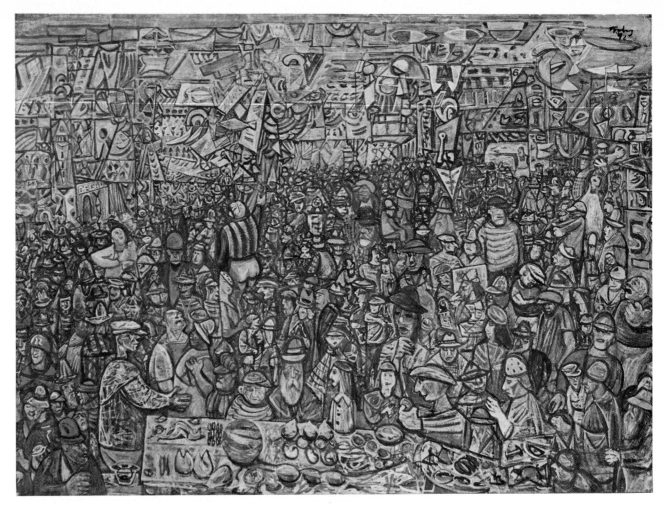

E Pluribus Unum. 1942 (or 1943). Tempera, 20¹/₈ × 24¹/₂″. Seattle Art Museum. Gift of Mrs. Thomas D. Stimson

THEMES AND SUBJECTS

MAN   *Every artist's problem today is "What will we do with the Human?"*[54]

Tobey's subjects are drawn from the totality of his ideas, beliefs, and experiences, even though they sometimes must take form in variations of a single brush movement. He is deeply concerned with the universal themes of man, nature, and God. Therefore, like many other modern painters who associate art with humanism, he has had to reconcile his movement toward abstractness with more than five millennia of figurative art. He has painted many self portraits. One of his youthful ambitions, barely abandoned even today, was to become a figure painter or sculptor.[55] In portraits, sketches, caricatures, religious compositions, or street scenes he has represented almost every social group and type: saints, society women, vendors and workers, actors and entertainers, dancers, prostitutes, and skid-row bums. His interest is never satiric, nor that of the "social realist," but it can become abstract: "Two men dressed in white jeans with white caps on their heads are climbing over a large sign of white letters. . . . What is important is their white, and the white of their letters."[56]

As a humanist, however, Tobey deplores the abstractness—aesthetic as well as technical and scientific—of modern life. Portraits are difficult to paint today, he says, "because we do not believe in man." With exhibitions as well as art schools in mind, he berates the "abstract academy," and paintings which are arresting but empty: "We're getting so abstract that we are practically Arabs. The whole Arab world, outside of Persia, is design in the abstract sense. Figuration is taboo." With these views, why did Tobey become a leader of the avant-garde? And why are Rothko, Lippold, and Mathieu among his favorite artists? The answer, which demonstrates how fully Tobey responds to the problems of his time, arises from his fourfold involvement with humanity, with nature, with the past, and with the future. The experimental temper projected him into new forms, as he has suggested, almost against his will. At one pole are his figure paintings; at the other are nonfigurative works: *City Radiance* (page 64) and *The Voice of the Doll* (page 34) were painted the same year. Because of the need to reconcile this conflict work by work, Tobey's development was slow and dialectical: "You see when I did all of these things nobody was doing them, and I had no support so I didn't know where I was, you see. And yet I had to do it, and I had a hard time, out of my love of figures, not to carry that along, because I like figures and I like people. . . ."

The portrait of Benjamin Kizer in 1950 (page 35), like that of Paul McCool in 1925 (page 90), embodies principles of representation hundreds of years old. Many con-

33

Worker. 1943. Tempera, 43×25″. Whereabouts unknown

Voice of the Doll. 1944. Tempera,
19¹/₂×7¹/₂″. Collection
Marian Willard Johnson, New York

temporary artists detach portraits from the evolution of their styles, but it is difficult for a painter who has experienced Cézanne and cubism to represent the figure with the organic autonomy it formerly had. For the contemporary, the pictorial rather than the human organism demands primary attention. Tobey responds to the humanism of Picasso's Blue and Rose Periods, and to the metaphysics and structure of cubism, but he cannot accept the dismemberment, deformation, and fragmentation of the figure for mere shape and pattern, or its devaluation into still life. "A terrible mutilation of the figure isn't very impressive either.... I've seen pictures in which the human figure has been chopped up, looked like leprosy, chewed to bits by dogs. This is not to me humanistic art at all." Tobey has broken up the figure in many ways; not always succesfully, but always with a related theme, as in *The Voice of the Doll,* one of his painted "comments": "This is where I think advertising ends—in rags and nothing." Certain early works, such as the dance mural for Dartington Hall (page 92), use emotional distortions of the figure resembling the frescoes of Orozco. More attuned to his mature style are compositions in which the solidity and autonomy of the body is maintained, but overlaid with a maze of lines or, as in *Family* (1949, page 68), immersed in a background that separates one part of the figure from another. There are many attempts to adjust calligraphic line to large figures: using loose brush drawing, a proletarian subject takes powerful but poetic form in *Worker* (1943, opposite); delicate "white writing" flattens plasticity in *Remembrance in Light* (1942, page 36).

Decreased in size and multiplied, small figures are easier to adjust to the new form and space. "Take the Renaissance," Tobey says, "the figure dominates the space. And then after the Renaissance, the space dominates the figure. In Oriental painting, the landscape dominates the figure." As he discovered by painful and sometimes unsuccessful experiments, multiple space demanded a new figure scale: "If you've experienced a new spatial thing, you can try to integrate the figure into it." In the early compartmented paintings, artifacts are as important as figures, for, as Tobey graphically—and in this case abstractly—shows in *Forms Follow Man* (1941, page 54) they surround human beings and migrate with them. Small objects and figures fit easily into compartments and interstices. In *Rummage, Threading Light,* and the Seattle and New York figure compositions, genre details make up a pictographic inventory of human needs and activities.

Probing but poetic in the genre pictures, Tobey's view of humanity tracks slowly backward and upward, taking in a larger and larger scene. He remembers evening

Portrait of Benjamin H. Kizer. (1950).
Tempera, $11\frac{1}{2} \times 7\frac{1}{8}''$.
Collection Carolyn Kizer, Seattle

crowds converging, like moths toward light, on the Café du Dôme or La Rotonde; two football teams intently struggling over one ball; crowds flowing like rivers between banks of steel, masonry, and glass; and the din of Hong Kong: "Thousands of Chinese characters are turning and twisting.... The narrow streets are alive in a way that Broadway isn't alive. Here all is human, even the beasts of burden. The human energy spills itself in multiple forms, writhes, sweats, and strains every muscle towards the day's bowl of rice. The din is terrific."[57] In Seattle, Tobey was himself a fixture of such a teeming environment, between 1940 and 1943, in the Pike Place

Public Market. Here, he constantly observed hawking merchants and grotesque shoppers; auctioneers, seamen, and cowpunchers; and vagrants who resembled birds and animals, and rolled themselves into balls to sleep (page 93). Since then he has been leading the fight to save the market from obliteration by "impersonal modernism" and "a world of automobiles."[58] In the paintings that resulted (page 32), these individual images are juxtaposed, compressed into patterns as flat as Indian designs, stretched or squeezed to fit each other, or dissolved in complexes of line and flurries of brush strokes.

Welcome Hero (page 60) and the other New York crowd scenes are different, for in them human movement is meshed with that of the metropolis. The mass of humanity and traffic epitomizes for Tobey America's dynamism and materialism, with an energy that is mechanical rather than human. He has painted New York more philosophically than Stella, Feininger, Marin, Davis, or Mondrian, with a profound sense of its interlocked lives, the boundlessness of its subterranean and aerial maze, and the complexity of its separations and interconnections. Its intensity is brought to a peak in *Flow of the Night* (1943, page 61) and *Broadway Boogie* (1942, page 26), which concentrates, at the lower center, on a grotesque head and a dancing figure, just as Ensor's *Entry of Christ into Brussels* (which Tobey did not see until 1958) focuses on the figure of Christ. From this center "emanates and flows the life which corresponds to that which they have built in the skies above them."[59] At a greater remove, and without figures, *City Radiance,* like *New York,* is a transparent crystal with an endlessly faceted extent, "a type of modern beauty I find only in the delicate structures of airplane beacons and electrical transformers and all that wonderful slender architecture connected with a current so potent and mysterious."[60] In another urban series, of which *New York Night* (1957) is a fine example, one sees the "shooting towers and space-eating lights" which to Tobey symbolize the age that, his criticisms and fears notwithstanding, is the greatest, the most radiant of all centuries.

Remembrance in Light. (1942). Tempera, 13³/8 × 9³/8". Collection Col. and Mrs. A. H. Hooker, Jr., Tacoma, Washington

Arena of Civilization. 1947. Tempera, 14 × 19³/₄″. Collection Mrs. Martha Jackson, New York

The full orchestra of Tobey's teleology is illustrated by *Arena of Civilization* (1947, page 37). It was first called "Breaking Parallels," and then "Lifting Parallels." The panel, divided like a Byzantine or Italian fresco or mosaic, is made up of superimposed compartments. At the bottom they seem subterranean, resembling Mithraea or catacombs, but above they become airier and more numerous. At the top they combine in a dome, which in turn opens onto the energized space above. One sees figures lying, sitting, and standing, seated on a rug like Moslems reading the Koran, or eating as in the Early Christian agape. From the lowest tier a swathed figure rises, like Lazarus from the tomb, to ascend toward another level, the floor of which opens to receive it. *Arena of Civilization* symbolizes Tobey's conviction that each cultural level, like each religion or style of art, is cradled in the womb of a previous state: "The medieval period grows out of the Roman period, and the basilica becomes the church."

Figuration ranges from realism to pure calligraphy in the closely packed *Pacific Transition* (1943, page 59). *Western Town* (1944, page 63) is a generalized city, where architecture dematerializes into the mist of a central vortex. The compartments appear densely populated. Above and toward the center the atmosphere is electric with presences, yet not a figure is depicted. *The Way* (1944, page 62) is even more evidently abstract, yet alive with figures, as Tobey says, "lost in space."

Tobey's paintings have been compared with aerial views, though his first airplane trip (which he found visually disappointing) was in 1962. His long-range view is conceptual rather than retinal. *Canal of Cultures*, and the related group of watercolors painted in 1950 and 1951 (page 70) observe humanity from the ultimate point of visibility: "I was thinking of how the cultures are only separated by canals. They are approaching each other, almost coexistent. . . ."

NATURE

While in Japan sitting on the floor of a room and looking over an intimate garden with flowers blooming and dragonflies hovering in space, I sensed that this small world almost under foot, shall I say, had a validity all its own . . . which must be realized and appreciated from its own level in space.[61]

If it were not for his absorption in human problems Tobey's attitude toward nature would approach that of Taoism and Zen. He has painted animals, fish, birds, and insects, and recalls a question of his friend Teng Kuei, who asked, one day while they were looking at an aquarium in a restaurant window: "Why do Western artists only paint a fish after it is dead?" He has painted gardens, trees, many kinds of landscape, dawn, dusk, and night. But Tobey's naturalism did not originate in Oriental influence; his tender feeling for natural states, birds, and animals began, as it will be shown, in childhood. But, even in the Oriental sense, Tobey is not a "landscape painter." As his comment on *Drift of Summer* (1942, page 57) emphasizes, he paints structures and processes: "Above and floating free above matted grasses, delicate thread-like structures rise and float, wind-blown as the summer passes."[62] Other images and titles relate to crystallization, drifting seeds or clouds, condensation, massing and dissolution. While painting he awaits the moment when (in the words of a Japanese friend) he can "get out of the way," and "let nature take over."[63]

The masterpiece of Tobey's nature paintings—a direct outcome of *Drift of Summer* and a prelude to the Meditative Series—is the great *Edge of August* (1953, opposite). The theme was in Tobey's mind for ten years before he could paint it successfully. Directly and without representation, as in music, this radical composition—"something that could shift out of sight, away"—recreates a last essence of peace and warmth: "*Edge of August* is

opposite: *Edge of August*. 1953. Tempera, 48 × 28″. The Museum of Modern Art, New York

trying to express the thing that lies between two conditions of nature, summer and fall. It's trying to capture that transition and make it tangible. Make it sing. You might say that it's bringing the intangible into the tangible."[64] The universe of the artist's consciousness is still permeated with delicate scents, pulsation, unnamable tactile sensations, and the murmur of movements audible only because of the silence around them. The iridescent field of minute calligraphy, modulating through the pale spectrum "that one sees around the moon," ends abruptly at the lower left—an area occupied in the later *Above the Earth V* (1956, page 77) by the quadrant of a sphere. The trembling cloud of writing is painted off the frame at the left, but at the right it fades into a dark void which represents, perhaps, the anxiety surrounding most moments of tranquility.

To anyone who has followed the pattern of Tobey's thinking and feeling, it will be evident that categories of subject must break down: Broadway is a river; cultures are separated by canals; a photograph of a crowd is a flower garden; a city is a crystal. As Gorky did, Tobey sees in visual metaphors. Because of this, and because Tobey is a symbolist, a series of intangible themes runs through his art that is independent of overt subject matter. *Light*, following its traditional symbolism, is associated with divinity, enlightenment, and spirituality. "Turner is greater than the Impressionists," in Tobey's mind, because "he dissolved everything into light."[65] Since 1920 Tobey has thought of light as structure. The Paris cafés of the twenties were "foci for people who wanted light to see in the night. They wanted light to sit in, to look at their friends, and talk...." Another of these themes—"operational," so to speak—is *migration:* the wandering of microscopic life, electricity, spores and seeds, birds and animals; of human beings and their thoughts, artifacts, art and architecture; of religions and cultures. Movement lines can indicate change from any one of these levels to others, or from one compartment of existence to another. Viewed symbolically in Tobey's mind, the breakup of Renaissance perspective and illusionism in favor of multiple space and moving focus is an historical parallel to the gradual dissolution of barriers between egos, nations, and cultures. When the level of vision rises and its horizon expands, so does the ethical consciousness. *Space* is for Tobey, as for many modern artists, a theme as well as an illusion of painting; the space in which we live every day, the blanket of atmospheric space around the earth, and the "inner space" conceived by the mind: "My imagination, it would seem, has its own geography."[66] *Scale* is also a theme: evident in the shift of magnitude from a crystal dish to a metropolis, or from a close-up to a telescopic view, and in the compression of encompassing concepts into tiny pictures. It is a question of the "scale of relativity": "I don't care if it's a picture eight feet high or eight inches high; to me it should have scale.... If it doesn't have that, then it's a repetition of experiences that are the same." In a similar sense, one can say that *unity* and *equilibrium* are subjects as well as conditions of Tobey's art.

In its essence, the movement of Tobey's mind is not simply migratory but anagogic, like that of medieval mysticism, from which it differs in drawing not from scholastic thought but from the complexity of modern experience. Perhaps more than any other modern artist —though one must compare Klee, Mondrian, Kandinsky, and Brancusi—Tobey has given form to mystical states, to worship. The texture, rhythm, and modes of formation of his *summa* are therefore at least as important as its content. Certain of his religious conceptions are represented; but more characteristically, experience is transmuted into form without an intermediary image. Transcendental human consciousness, it could be said, is Tobey's ultimate theme. Those pictures which convey it directly are his best answer to the coarse assertion that only the depiction of flesh is "humanistic." If man is a part of nature, Tobey says, "a landscape can be humanistic.... Can the human be seen in the abstract? Saint Francis is a vertical. Humanism is not just figuration. The 'return to the figure' does not make you a humanist. It may make you an anti-humanist."

THE FORMATION OF TOBEY'S STYLE

An artist must find his expression closely linked to his individual experience or else follow in the old grooves resulting in lifeless forms.[67]

In the preceding chapters Tobey's art and ideas were discussed with little consideration for their long period of gestation and formation, even though he was forty-five years old before their diverse elements began to coalesce. Before that time, though there are fine and even masterful pictures, his production is contradictory in style and uneven in quality. Erratic, but logical in retrospect, Tobey's path was a rigorous discipline as well as a self-conducted apprenticeship. The events that directed him were as varied as the paintings, many of them dispersed or destroyed, that punctuate his phases. Artists have two biographies: one made up of the same personal events as the lives of nonartists, and another contained in a different order of time – a ladder of reflection and illumination like that ascended by a philosopher or a mystic.[68] Tobey has always felt that the artist's role was "to be a filter of life, so that other people could see what that condensation is." His "inner" biography, moreover, is of special interest because its expansion from isolation to internationalism, and from illustration to inspired abstraction, shows little resemblance to the pattern, varied though it is, by which Western artists are most often trained.

In the pages that follow, crucial stages and moments in the formation of Tobey's style are isolated from his biography as one might select certain sequences from a film. These begin with Tobey's childhood, and end in 1935, with the event that separates his years of preparation from his years of fulfillment.

Middle West. (1929). Oil on canvas, 37³/₄ × 59³/₄″. Seattle Art Museum. Gift of Mrs. Thomas D. Stimson

THE MIDDLE WEST

> *Wisconsin is far away. The Wisconsin in my mind is often very far away. It comes back sometimes by itself like a wandering dog.*[69]

Tobey's childhood was passed in Wisconsin and Indiana, at the cultural – albeit not the geographical – midpoint of the continent. *Middle West* (above), painted more than twenty years after the impressions it recalls, represents a land untouched by international currents. On a bare plain a highway and a railroad line, like the jet strips of a modern airport, sweep toward the four winds. Here is the point of origin, as it were, of Tobey's global migrations. Happy to say, nature and life are an artist's primary sources, so a childhood innocent of art can provide its raw material. The impressions that guide Tobey's brush today may have confronted his senses ten, twenty, or sixty years before. Thus in 1951 he can summon up images

not seen since he lived the life of Tom Sawyer in Wisconsin: of the Mississippi, "level and motionless"; of leaves being raked "under the great elms darkening in the evening light"; of a beloved cave, hard to reach on the banks above the river. His eyes widen with childlike wonder when he recalls that Indians still lived in wigwams near his home, and he can still see the Indian mounds near the river: "rounded forms full of fantastic objects never found." He remembers the Egyptian yellow lotus on Trempealeau Bay, "the first crocus," and the care with which he brought home and planted wildflowers; and later, at Hammond High School in Indiana, the dead sparrow that only he, among the students, cared to preserve and stuff. He can still see the image of a train on the Minnesota side of the river, crossing his window like a toy, and hear the sound of its whistle. Once it has passed "the night breathes in silence – breathes to the moon, to space mysterious and tantalizing."[70] It was as a child that Tobey first experienced a sense of oneness with nature, and a consequent feeling for the sacredness and mystery of life: "My whole early experience until I was sixteen," he says, "was just purely nature. Not the mind at all, just nature."

An artist's inherent traits must be seen as directives which mediate each influence or choice that contributes to his unique expression. Tobey's mother called him "the most restless young'un I ever had." Ever since, his sensibility has remained mobile and impatient, always searching out some untried channel from one condition of being or feeling to another, always moving back and forth in time and space. It is difficult to ascertain the source of a religious sense, but of Tobey it can surely be said that it was instilled early. In his words: "I got my religion like my hair."[71] His education, like that of Rembrandt or van Gogh, began in a devout Protestant home; the art of all three later expands toward human, mystical, and philosophical breadth. It was a family circle to which the idea of art was foreign. But Tobey's mother loved to make beautiful things, and George Tobey, who was a builder, felt a real responsibility to encourage his younger son's talent. Mark rejected the building trade that led his brother Leon, ten years his elder, to become a designer of roof structures; but Tobey's later absorption in structure surely reflects this influence. From his father he also learned the opposite of structural form: he vividly remembers the rounded forms of animals that George Tobey drew with a thick carpenter's crayon, or carved in Indian red pipestone. His father also bought him tools of art, such as they were, and later even sent him twelve miles to a few classes at the Art Institute of Chicago.

On the borderline between childhood and the first glimmer of what art could be, lies an experience at the Saturday class which Tobey calls his "first lesson in relativity": "We had a still-life setup to paint. Suddenly I saw that the pitcher was *so* big and the glass was *so* big. From that time on everything was all right. But I experienced it myself."[72]

THE HANDLING BUG

Wisconsin is before Chicago, and Harrison Fisher is before Michelangelo.[73]

The Art Institute of Chicago was, for Tobey at least, the only place where influences from the East moved "circularly" into the Middle West and then returned from whence they came. But in 1909, when the Tobey family moved to Chicago, they were too poor for Mark to augment his few art lessons by regular enrollment at the Institute. It is unlikely, however, that he would have been a docile student. From the Saturday class he cites with amusement the teacher's criticism of a landscape he was painting: "You can't have a pink sky in the West, it's too far from the sun." He is dismayed, in retrospect, that the only creative freedom was in the "composition" course for students in their last year. "The imagination can be murdered without sentence," Tobey wrote in 1951 of art teaching: "The walls are hung with painted corpses. . . . Why don't art schools have classes on how to remain aware?"[74] But one professor, "old Reynolds," from whom Tobey had a criticism or two, showed real insight when he observed that his student had been infected by "the American handling bug" – that is to say he preferred flashy brush technique to the tedium of careful modeling.

As he approached twenty, Tobey wanted to be an illustrator. After being fired from jobs as a blueprint boy and a letterer – for lack of interest in the first case and poor work in the second – he made a quick success rendering the faces of pretty girls, on the production line of a cheap fashion studio. During lunch hours and after work he pored over *The Saturday Evening Post* and other "cover girl" publications, which he collected, to become so conversant with the styles of the illustrators that a detail was sufficient for him to recognize their brush mannerisms (page 88). His heroes were Harrison Fisher, Howard Chandler Christy, and J. C. Leyendecker who "for sheer technique took the cake." For Tobey, at twenty, "the American girl was the most beautiful thing you could put on canvas." He looked backward, also, to the already fading image – willowy, coy, and soft-coifed – of the "Gibson girl." In reverie he still sees her face "in the moon."[75]

Tobey pictures his early education in the astronomical images of Bahá'í. A new master rose "above the horizon" of his consciousness. Frederic Remington, he recalls, "flashed like a comet before my eyes."[76] Yet he learned of great painters as well as illustrators. One day in the studio a fashion artist dropped some cheap reproductions of Raphael, Rembrandt, and Michelangelo on Tobey's drawing table with the challenge: "Why don't you paint something out of your own noodle? Why be a monkey?" A lady "who had been in Paris" introduced him to the paintings of Sorolla at the Art Institute. His brilliant brushwork, like that of Sargent, whom Tobey had also discovered, stirred him with admiration; then the "Hals brush was lashed to Sargent's as the 'handling bug' bit deeply into all those like myself."[77] At this same time, an elderly Swiss friend took Tobey to a German bookstore where, in the magazines *Simplicissimus* and *Jugend*, he saw drawings and paintings by von Stuck, von Lenbach, and Leo Putz. The linear undulations and floriform naturalism of art nouveau may well have influenced early works such as *Before Form* (1929, page 48); swirling, wavelike rhythms recur thereafter in countless variations.

Neither cover girls nor Remington cowpunchers turn up later in Tobey's painting, but the obsession with the brush, on the other hand, is an essential link between his insular youth in Chicago and the internationalized expression of his maturity. He already knew something of the monumental light and shade of Michelangelo and Raphael, and of Titian's color. In the divergence of his enthusiasms, Tobey had stumbled on the dualism by which Western painting has evolved: the inherent opposition of "painterly" to "sculptural" style. When he boarded the train in 1911 in quest of success as a fashion illustrator in New York, a soothsayer with a knowledge of art history might have foreseen that Tobey was to relive the dilemma that was canonized in the seventeenth century by the debates between the "Rubenists" and "Poussinists."

THE BAHÁ'Í WORLD FAITH

The years between Tobey's first move to New York and his teaching appointment at the Cornish School in Seattle, in 1922, were a substitute for the academic training he had missed. Limited but real successes – as an illustrator, charcoal portraitist, decorator, and caricaturist – added practice and professionalism to natural aptitude. That the expanse of his horizon was still narrow, at least in 1913, is established by his complete incomprehension, when he visited the great "Armory Show" in Chicago, not only of recent paintings such as Duchamp's *Nude Descending a Staircase*,[78] but also of Cézanne, van Gogh, and post-impressionism in general. Tobey's first one-man show, of charcoal portraits, was held in 1917 at M. Knoedler and Company, New York. These drawings are now dispersed, but a self-portrait of that year shows the skill of hand, clarity of thought, and acuteness of observation which gave Tobey success as a self-trained portraitist. Except for the pupils of the eyes, all reference to color value – i.e., the tonal difference between violet and yellow – is carefully excluded in the interest of clear definition and solidity.

The exhibition had been arranged by Marie Sterner, who introduced Tobey to a portrait painter, Juliet Thompson, for whom he agreed to pose. During these sittings he learned that she was a follower of the Bahá'í World Faith, and he became interested in the religious literature in her studio. As a result Tobey was invited to visit a Bahá'í camp in Maine where, though he did not fully understand the doctrine, he gained a faith that has since governed his life: "I just got it in here, you know, and I said: 'Well, this is the truth.' So that was that." Without doubt, this was the crucial spiritual redirection of Tobey's life and of his development as an artist. Its importance for his world view has been discussed in some detail (pages 9–14), and its immediate effect on his art can be ascertained by the *Conflict of the Satanic and Celestial Egos* (page 10), painted not long after his conversion, and a self-portrait of the early twenties (page 90).

Between 1919 and 1921–in direct contradiction to his sculptural predisposition–Tobey reacted strongly against "the Renaissance sense of space and order," feeling that forms "should be freer and not so separated from the space around them,"[79] though he had little idea of how such a transformation could be accomplished, and little knowledge of the European precedents to which he might otherwise have turned. "As I remember," he recalls, "I really wanted to smash form, to melt it in a more moving and dynamic way";[80] "I wanted to smash this image that was in space and I wanted to give the light that was in the form in space a release." Unfortunately the works that would demonstrate this new attitude–one called *Descent into Form* and some studies "full of minute forms or patterns"–are lost.

Beside the spiritualizing influence of Bahá'í the dynamism of New York, which Marin and Stella had already painted, must also have played a part in Tobey's desire to liberate and activate form, though it was not revealed in his painting, except for realistic studies such as *Burlesque* (1924), until 1935. He remembers the 1920 as the "welcome hero" period. Their emotional impact is recreated in a recollection of his experiences on November 11, 1918. Early in the day his friend Janet Flanner appeared at his Washington Square studio and announced: "Mark, the war is over." Together they went into the streets and mingled with the milling crowds: "You know, everything went wild," Tobey recalls. "That's the only time I was ever lost in a fog. Whatever I did that entire day I haven't any idea but I know what it is to have no consciousness at all and be in a fog." These years were for him a montage of "sirens, dynamic lights, brilliant parades and returning heroes. An age of confusion and stepped-up rhythms."[81] For one familiar with the New York paintings it is unnecessary to labor the importance of experiences like this. And even in the abstract pictures of the fifties Tobey's space is filled with strokes like confetti or tape floating over a parade. In 1962, after watching the *adventus* of the astronaut John Glenn on television, Tobey joked, as he does while leafing through picture magazines or driving through an industrial panorama: "I never saw so many Tobeys." But it is always first impressions, through all the senses, that have precedence in his memory, however long it may take for them to re-emerge in painting. Repeated impressions can be superfluous, and, since by then first have been heightened and assimilated, are often disappointing.[82]

THE "PERSONAL DISCOVERY OF CUBISM"

Tobey arrived in Seattle from New York in 1922, and began teaching, with a class of four pupils, at a progressive school of the arts directed by Miss Nellie Cornish. The event was fortunate on both sides. For the city, the ultimate outcome was an internationally known regional school of painting in a previously unproductive region.

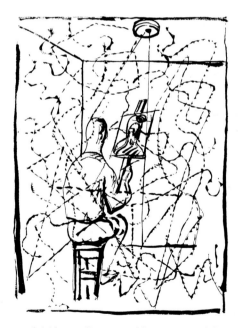

Mark Tobey's diagram of his "personal discovery of cubism." Done in New York, 1962.

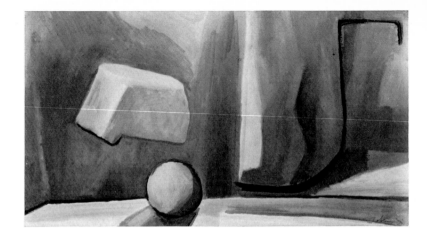

Table and Ball. 1936. Tempera,
10¹/₂ × 19¹/₂″. Seattle Art Museum.
Eugene Fuller Memorial Collection

For Tobey (though the cultural vacuum he found was disappointing) the greater human warmth, the slower pace, and the expanding spatiality of the magnificent landscape had a strong appeal. Teaching, moreover, was an enriching experience of which he still speaks with pleasure, regretting the impatience and eagerness for quick success that makes young artists today less and less willing to work under a master.

As in everything else, Tobey's mode of teaching – "a sort of receptive method" – was his own. For children, Tobey's advice to anxious parents was: "Just give them materials and be interested in art yourselves."[83] Older students were told to "start with the imagination," and then "go out and look at things, to study them, and that will stimulate your retentive memory and your retentive memory will bring it back in your imagination again." Fearful beginners were told to begin right where they were: "'I can't make the figure.' 'All right. Can you make a black dot?' 'Yes.' 'Can you extend it down?' 'Yes.' 'Can you extend it up?' 'Yes.' 'Can you extend it a little more? Can you put another dot?... All right, you've got a figure. That's the thick part of the arm; that's the thick part of the leg. That's the thinner part of the arm; that's the thinner part of the leg. This connects with this; that with

that.'" Tobey confesses that his un-Western ideographic approach to representation was in part necessitated by his ignorance of standard art school disciplines but adds: "Those people never forgot my teaching and I never forgot it either." Later he discovered a similar method being practiced in the universities of Northern India.

Tobey's own development was closely linked with his teaching; the need to back up his conclusions led him, for the first time, to analyze the work of many artists, among them Cézanne, Braque, and Picasso. He had seen cubism, of course, but had not understood it. One result of this research was what Tobey now calls his "personal discovery of cubism." One night at the Cornish School he pictured himself, in his mind, working in a small centrally illuminated room. Within this compartment a portrait on an easel before him formed a second smaller compartment of space. Next he imagined a fly moving freely around him and the objects in the room. It was able to move up or down, and in any other direction, to light on the artist's back, head or hand, on the ceiling, wall or floor, and then to take off in another direction. As the path of movement crossed and recrossed around the central axis, it generated a complex of line, and by its many crossings, imaginary planes and shapes. Although related to the objects in the room, this secondary matrix of form was independent of them, and was entirely the product of movement.

What Tobey had conceived, but did not make use of until many years later was, precisely, the structural "animation of space" that underlies most of his mature painting. His cubism was a major step toward the ultimate interpenetration of mass and void. Afterward he could see solid objects, such as those abstractly represented in *Table and Ball* (1936, opposite), as transparent and metaphysical: "I don't need to bother about that solid there.... I can go right through myself and I get here and come up there.... When I got through with this, I was freed from the cube. But it was my own personal experience." Another conclusion, more truly "cubist" than the paintings of Picasso and Braque, was that "all life is six-sided, so it's all cubic. Even a piece of paper has six sides; my finger does; my hand does. Everything is six-sided." Almost more important, the principle of moving line was inaugurated. The path of an imaginary fly was to become a metaphysical symbol.

TENG KUEI

The freely moving brush was the second discovery Tobey made in Seattle. In 1923 he began to learn the technique of Chinese calligraphy from Teng Kuei, a young Chinese artist studying at the University of Washington. It was an experience for which Tobey had been prepared by his early infection with "the handling bug" and his subsequent conversion to Bahá'í, with its doctrine of union between East and West: "All is in motion now. A design of flames encircles the quiet Buddha. One step backward into the past and the tree in front of my studio in Seattle is all rhythm, lifting, springing upward!

"I have just had my first lesson in Chinese brush from my friend and artist Teng Kuei. The tree is no more a solid in the earth, breaking into lesser solids bathed in chiaroscuro. There is pressure and release. Each movement, like tracks in the snow, is recorded and often loved for itself. The Great Dragon is breathing sky, thunder, and

shadow; wisdom and spirit vitalized."[84] What Tobey learned from Teng Kuei, but did not apply until later, was "the difference between volume and the living line" – a means of opening solid form, giving tangibility to empty space, and of breathing life into static Western realism.

Of course Seattle gave Tobey many things other than these peak experiences. He was aware of the closeness of the Orient which, in San Francisco, came "rolling in with the tides."[85] But Seattle seemed pocketed. "I have often thought that if the West Coast had been open to aesthetic influence from Asia, as the East Coast was to Europe," Tobey wrote in 1957, "what a rich nation we would be!"[86] More keenly than Seattle's proximity to the Orient he felt the broad sweep of mountains, sea, and forest surrounding the city, and the need for "uplift work" which "begins when you leave Grand Central Station."[87] Psychologically the only exit from Seattle, Tobey felt, was toward Alaska. He became a collector of the carving, weaving, and painting of the Northwest Coast Indians. As works like *Drums, Indians and the Word of God* (page 66) attest, Indian art made a mark on his own.

DARTINGTON HALL

In an article published in Seattle in 1931 mourning Tobey's departure for England he is described as "the stepson of the furies," as "the most vital personality I have seen," whose "emotion blows hot, blows cold," but is never calm.[88] He must have been a dashing and commanding figure. But as his second New York exhibition, held at Romany Marie's Café Gallery in 1929, verifies, his painting was not yet mature. The catalogue alleged him to be a surrealist, but realistic paintings like *Middle West* hung beside undulating abstractions (page 48), and still life beside bizarre fantasies. This was the exhibition of an individualistic and experimental artist who, though he had traveled extensively and had lived in both New York and Paris, was not in touch with avant-garde art. As the first major article on Tobey (written in 1930 by Muriel Draper) states, in the twenties he did caricatures, illustrations, portraits, still life, wood and clay sculpture, landscapes, mural de-

Before Form. (1929). Oil, $33^{1}/_{4} \times 44^{1}/_{2}''$.
Collection Mrs. Horton C. Force, Seattle

Modal Tide. (1940). Oil, $34^{1}/_{2} \times 47^{3}/_{8}''$. Seattle Art Museum

sign, and abstraction. He worked in almost every painting medium, and on any kind of support that was at hand. His prodigious gift had not yet been disciplined and channeled, and some of his most concentrated art, as Miss Draper properly states, tended toward "intellectualized philosophy in paint."[89]

Dartington Hall, a school and cultural center in Devonshire, some 200 miles from London, was Tobey's home between 1930 and 1938. Here he taught, and met such artists and intellectuals as Aldous Huxley, Pearl Buck, Arthur Waley, and Rudi Shankar, all devoted, as Tobey was, to a marriage of Eastern and Western ideas. According to Janet Flanner, Dartington Hall "was the center of the most importance educative experiments of this period."[90] The school was housed in a venerable monument of English architecture, and set in a grove where it seemed "that Pan still lived behind the old oak trees."[91] Tobey found in Devonshire a haven away from the clamor of New York and the provincialism of America. "The nights were so silent you could hear the horses breathing." "My ideal of life," he said in 1962, "would be – well, if not the portico of the philosophers – at least learning amidst trees. I mean an ideal setting of nature and yet the finest core of men's minds. . . ." Dartington Hall was the sanctuary from which Tobey left, sponsored by Mr. and Mrs. Leonard Elmhurst (who supported the school), for his crucial visit to China and Japan in 1934, and it was at Dartington Hall that, after returning the next year, his distinctive style originated.

CHINA AND JAPAN

Tobey stayed with the family of his friend Teng Kuei in Shanghai, living the ordinary life of the city. He became familiar with native foods, amusements, theaters and concerts; he looked at painting and sculpture, and met artists and musicians. In careful detail, his experiences are recorded in his diary. Later he traveled alone to Japan, where he saw No drama, Kabuki, Japanese painting and flower arrangement. He passed a month in a Zen monastery in Kyoto talking with the abbots and monks, at-

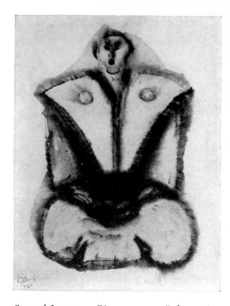

Seated Japanese Figure. 1934. Ink, 14³/₄ × 11¹/₂". Seattle Art Museum. Eugene Fuller Memorial Collection

China. 1934. Ink, 9¹/₂ × 7¹/₄". Collection Mr. and Mrs. Max Weinstein, Seattle

49

tempting Eastern meditation, practicing calligraphy, and painting. Day after day he studied a sumi painting of a large free-brush circle: "Was it selflessness? Was it the Universe – where I could lose my identity?"[92] He practiced painting before a moon window through which everything was framed in a circle, and composed poetry in the Haiku form. Tobey did not achieve enlightenment – satori – and doubts if any American, or even any modern Japanese artist has done so. Nor does he claim a full understanding of Zen. But it reinforced his conviction that "if you wish to break down the rational mind and to reveal what is behind it, you must pass through the experience of having it smashed." He found Zen released him, by its "circle of emptiness,"[93] from the domination of others' ideas; and he took as his own the Japanese emphasis on conservation and concentration, simplicity, directness, and profundity. He prefers the Japanese aesthetic to the Chinese, and values the ideal of *shibui*, which to him means hidden beauty: "that which doesn't look like anything, but in time discloses its jewels." He accepts the idea

of accident, and especially the freedom of the "flung" style, which he used so magnificently in his sumis: "When I get into the old Zen monks who did calligraphy, then I'm very happy." Most important, China and Japan gave the final encouragement to Tobey's natural "writing impulse," and to his idea that forms could migrate from Orient to Occident just as they previously had in the opposite direction.

Bahá'í and Zen were Tobey's two most important spiritual influences; but Bahá'í, as he says, "found him," whereas it was he who sought out and found Zen. "I could never be anything," he confesses, "but the occidental I am."[94]

BROADWAY NORM

In a San Francisco hotel room, on his way back to England from Japan, Tobey painted a series of "the animal world under the influence of moonlight," of which *Three Birds* (below) is typical. They were a prime source for Graves, Callahan, and other painters of the later "North-

Broadway Norm. 1935. Tempera, 13¼ × 9⅜″. Collection Carol Ely Harper, Seattle

left: *Three Birds.* 1934(?). Tempera, 10¾ × 14⅞″. Seattle Art Museum. Eugene Fuller Memorial Collection

west School," but are in no way calligraphic, resembling Chinese or cubist bronzes. Strange as it may seem, Tobey even then had not applied his training in direct brush composition to his major painting. But one evening in the fall of 1935, after he had returned to the quiet of Devonshire, he began to improvise a little picture made up of a mesh of whitish lines on a brown background, with a scattering of small forms in blue and other colors showing through the network. It was like a collection of objects in a crystal dish, and anything but Oriental in appearance. In a sudden, instinctive flash back, the image became, not Japan, but New York: he "realized that it was Broadway, with all the people caught in the lights."[95] Such was the unpremeditated realization, Tobey explains, through which "the calligraphic impulse I had received in China enabled me to convey, without being bound by forms, the motion of people and the cars and the whole vitality of the scene."[96] *Broadway Norm* (left), as the little painting was later titled, is not impressive; like the neck of an hourglass, however, it separates Tobey's earlier period of dispersion, migration, and search, from maturity. After 1935, no matter how widely one work may differ from another, they all gather around a common center. *Broadway* (page 16), already studied in some detail, was painted a night or two later, and *Welcome Hero* (also called *The 1920s*, page 60), the night after that.[97] Its subject goes back to the early years in New York that Tobey remembers so vividly, and to the reception of Lindbergh after his transatlantic flight. "Multiple space" and "moving focus" were already inaugurated in *Welcome Hero*. As has already been indicated, it went further than *Broadway*, fulfilling the early desire to "smash" form by breaking apart the perspective focus and all but reversing the yin-yang of full and empty volume, flatness and depth. So shocked was Tobey by his unplanned breakthrough that, as he painted *Welcome Hero*, in which every major postulate of his development fell together as in a catastrophe, he shook with fear. The Eastern dragon had been harnessed to Western dynamism.

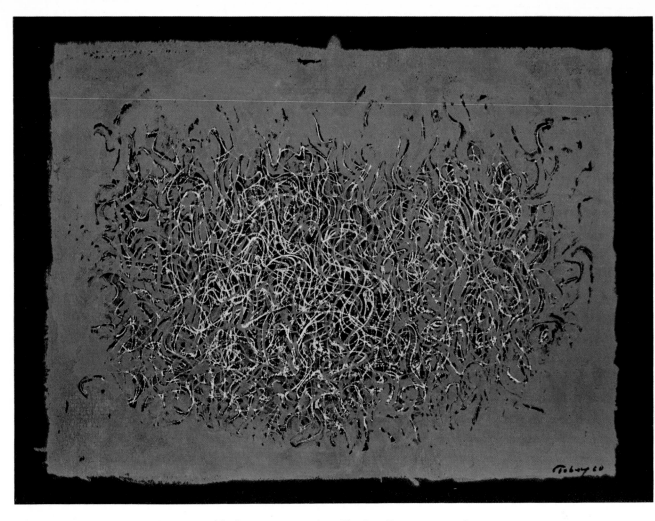

Homage to Rameau. 1960. Tempera on black paper, 6³/₄ × 8″. Willard Gallery, New York

SUMMARY COMMENT

A power to absorb and symbolize the discrepant realities of an entire period has been a sign of greatness in an artist from the time of Phidias to that of Cézanne and Picasso. Tobey's structures of lines, strokes, and signs have this kind of inclusiveness: they are seismographic records of the contemporary mind and sensibility as it responds to the delights, dangers, staggering challenges, and unprecedented potentialities of life in our time. There are of course significant aspects of human experience that find no place in his art, but it is amazing to comprehend the breadth of compass this profound painter has achieved. He has been consistently led to draw a greater diversity of meaning into the distilled sphere of his art. In a new temporal and geographic context, Tobey's aim is identical with that attributed by George Rowley to Confucianism and Taoism, the two modes of thought that lie behind Chinese painting: "They both sought 'inner reality' in a fusion of opposites."[98] Followed to their universal meeting ground, many of the polarities that Rowley discovered in Oriental painting – spirit and matter, divine and human, personal and impersonal, man and nature, tradition and originality, expansion and contraction, delicacy and power, improvisation and preparation – are also among those that make up Tobey's content and form.

Even in more specific characteristics, Tobey's equilibrium derives from a yin-yang of contradictions. In the geography of ideas, he came from nowhere. His speech, mannerisms, and many of his tastes are Midwestern. Much of his subject matter is as Yankee, in its own way, as that of Sheeler, Hopper, or Curry. He is the founding master of the "Northwest School" of painting. Yet at the same time Tobey may well be the most internationally minded painter of importance in the history of art. What could better illustrate his increasing internationalism than the evolution of his idea of line and brush? It began with the ornamental embellishments of Harrison Fisher and other cover-girl specialists, progressed to *Jugendstil* and the bravura of Sargent and Sorolla, expanded to include Hals, and finally came to encompass most of the world's calligraphic art, and great Eastern masters like Liang K'ai and Sesshu. What an unprecedented fusion of perspectives!

Tobey is a humanist, a traditionalist, a lover of the body as a subject and humanity as a theme. Nevertheless – under the influence of modern existence rather than modern art – he was led to fragment, obscure, and ultimately to dematerialize the human form and image entirely, in search of a valid expression of the human spirit. Belatedly but by sheer awareness of modern life, he found himself projected to the apex of contemporary abstract style.

Art is the center of Tobey's activity. Like facets of the visible environment, therefore, his ethical, philosophical, and religious convictions should perhaps be regarded only as components and sources. Yet it is hard to ignore Tobey the social critic, religious reformer, or even the prophet. His adoption of free brush as a means was not a technical coup but a philosophical conclusion. Long before the world was polarized into two nuclear arsenals, Tobey knew that the hiatus between East and West should be closed. Contracting the globe to eye-range, he foretold and led the aesthetic counterrotation of the world which is now bringing into balance forces that have indeed met like "long-lost lovers."[99]

In Tobey's philosophy there is no break between aesthetic and political imperatives: the ego must soften and open; baneful divisions must be bridged; misunderstandings must be resolved. If society is to avoid a catastrophe, the consciousness of man must be universalized. Equilibrium is as necessary in life as in painting. The world must become one. For Tobey one great need, if this fulfillment is to be realized, is the reconciliation of science with religion.

These two paths toward truth, one ancient and the other modern, do not yet meet. Is it possible that they can be reconciled, if at all, only through art?

Rummage. 1941. Tempera, $38^3/8 \times 25^7/8''$.
Seattle Art Museum. Eugene Fuller Memorial Collection

right: *Forms Follow Man.* (1941). Tempera, $13^5/8 \times 19^5/8''$.
Seattle Art Museum. Eugene Fuller Memorial Collection

Threading Light. 1942. Tempera, $29^3/_8 \times$ $19^1/_2''$. The Museum of Modern Art, New York

Transition to Forms.
1942. Tempera, 28×22″.
Destroyed by fire

Drift of Summer. 1942.
Tempera, 28×22″.
Collection Wright Ludington,
Santa Barbara, California

Gothic. 1943. Tempera, 27³/₄ × 21⁵/₈″. Collection Berthe Poncy
Jacobson, Seattle

Western Splendor. 1943. Tempera, 26³/₄ × 19¹/₄″. Collection Mr.
and Mrs. Roe Duke Watson, Seattle

Pacific Transition. 1943. Tempera, 23¹/₄ × 31¹/₄". City Art Museum of St. Louis

Welcome Hero (The 1920s).
(1935?). Tempera, 26 × 19″.
Destroyed by fire

Flow of the Night. 1943. Tempera, 20³/4 × 15¹/2″. Portland Art Museum, Portland, Oregon

The Way. 1944. Tempera, 13⁷/₈ × 22¹/₈″. Collection Mrs. Albert H. Newman, Chicago

Western Town. 1944. Tempera, $12 \times 18^{3}/4''$.
Collection Mr. and Mrs. Paul Feldenheimer,
Portland, Oregon

Remote Field. 1944. Tempera, pencil
and crayon, $28^{1}/8 \times 30^{1}/8''$.
The Museum of Modern Art, New York.
Gift of Mr. and Mrs. Jan de Graaff

Lines of the City. 1945. Tempera, 17¹/₂×21³/₄″. Addison Gallery of American Art, Phillips Academy, Andover, Massachusetts

right: *City Radiance.* 1944. Tempera, 19³/₈×14¹/₄″. Collection Mrs. Lyonel Feininger, New York (detail page 22)

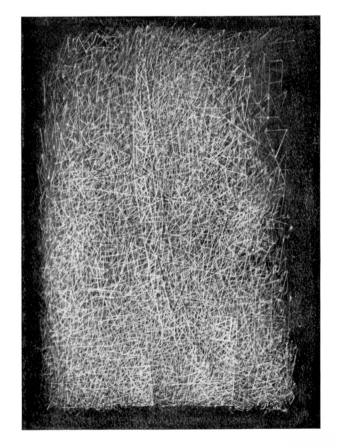

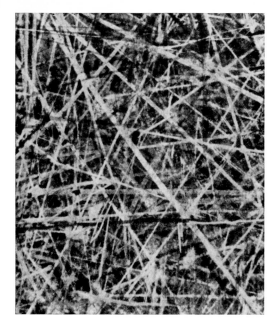

right: *New York*. 1944. Tempera, 33 × 21″.
Collection Marian Willard Johnson, New York
(detail above)

Drums, Indians and the Word of God. 1944. Tempera, $18^{1}/_{2} \times$ $13^{7}/_{8}''$. Herman Shulman Collection

Tropicalism. 1948. Oil and tempera, $26^{1}/_{2} \times 19^{3}/_{4}''$. Galerie Saqqârah, Gstaad, Switzerland (detail page 22)

Delta. 1952. Oil and tempera, $43^{1}/_{2} \times 27^{5}/_{8}''$.
Collection Dan R. Johnson, New York

The Deposition. 1947. Tempera, 15¹/₂ × 11³/₈″. Collection Mr. and Mrs. George C. Miyake, Seattle

Family. 1949. Tempera, 12 × 7¹/₂″. Collection Marian Willard Johnson, New York

Homage to the Virgin. 1948. Tempera, 9 × 15″. Collection Mr. and Mrs. Daniel Saidenberg, New York

above: *Canal of Cultures*. 1951. Tempera, 19¹/₂ × 25³/₄″.
Collection Benjamin H. Kizer, Spokane, Washington

right: *Aerial City*. 1950. Watercolor, 16¹/₈ × 19³/₄″.
Collection Mrs. Lyonel Feininger, New York

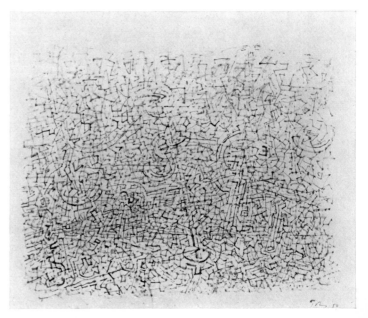

Written Over the Plains. 1950. Oil and tempera, 29⁷/₈ × 39⁵/₈″.
San Francisco Museum of Art. Gift of Mrs. Ferdinand Smith

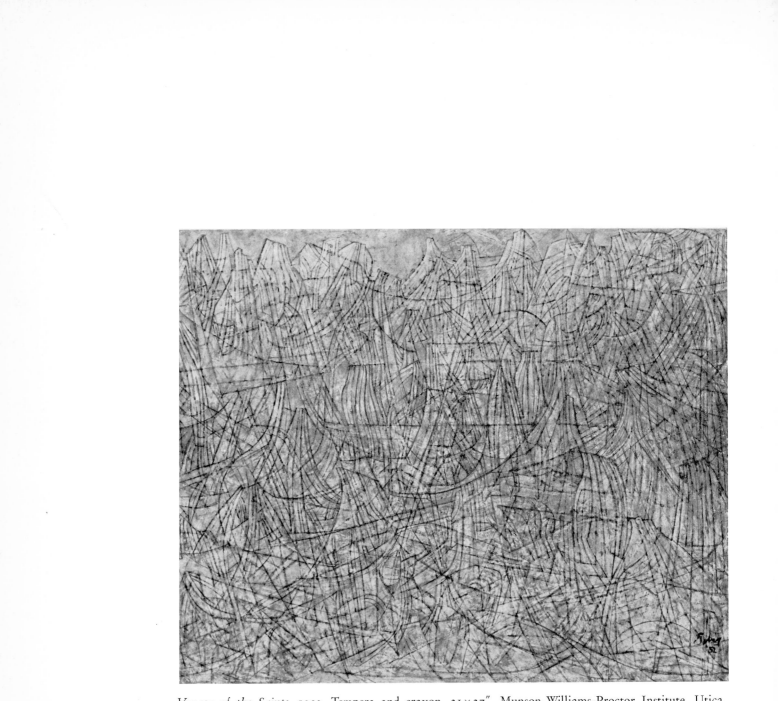

Voyage of the Saints. 1952. Tempera and crayon, $21 \times 27''$. Munson-Williams-Proctor Institute, Utica, New York. Edward W. Root Bequest

Medieval Landscape. 1958. Tempera, 17 × 34⅝″. Collection N. Richard Miller, New York

1951. 1951. Tempera, 43³/₄ × 27³/₄″. Collection
Mr. and Mrs. Joseph R. Shapiro, Oak Park, Illinois

The Avenue. 1954. Tempera and watercolor, 40 × 30¹/₄″.
Norton Gallery and School of Art, West Palm Beach, Florida

opposite: *Above the Earth*. 1953. Tempera, 39¹/₄ × 29³/₄″.
The Art Institute of Chicago. Gift of Mr. and Mrs. Sigmund
Kunstadter

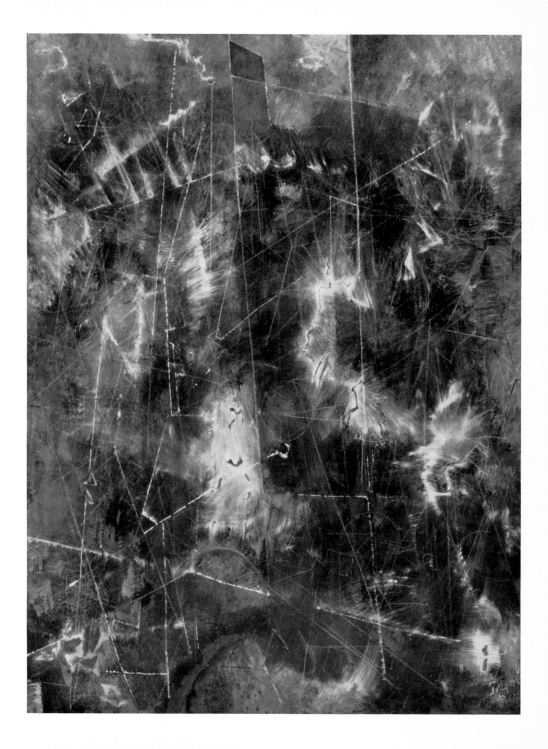

Meditative Series VIII. 1954.
Tempera, 17³/₄ × 11³/₄″. Collection
Mr. and Mrs. Arthur L. Dahl,
Pebble Beach, California

76

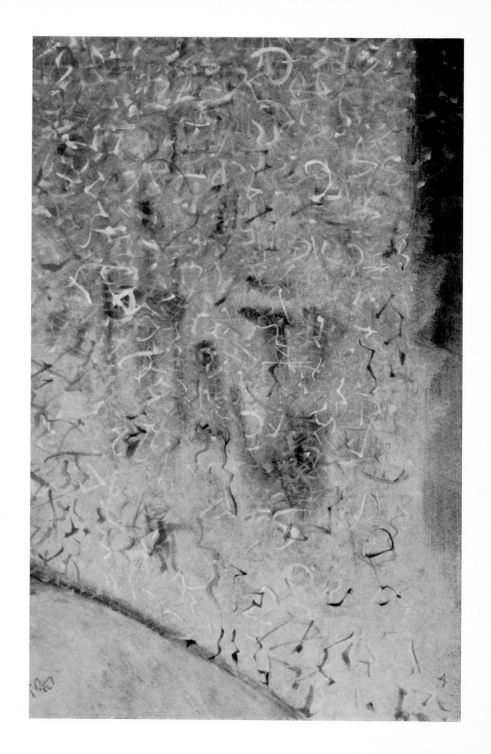

Above the Earth V. 1956.
Tempera, $18 \times 11^{3}/_{4}''$. Collection
Mr. and Mrs. Richard Lippold,
Locust Valley, New York

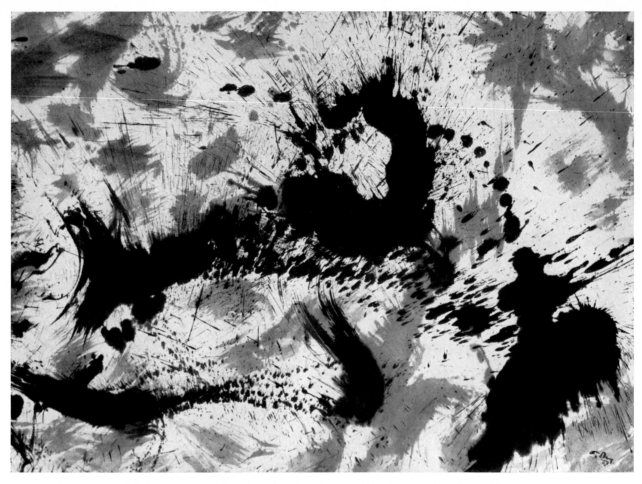

Dragonade. 1957. Sumi (ink), 24³/₈ × 34¹/₈″. Milwaukee Art Center. Gift of Mrs. Edward R. Wehr

Space Ritual XIII. 1957. Sumi (ink),
50³/₈ × 26¹/₄″. Willard Gallery, New York

79

Jeweled Jungle. 1958. Tempera and ink, 9¹/₄ × 13³/₄″. Willard Gallery, New York

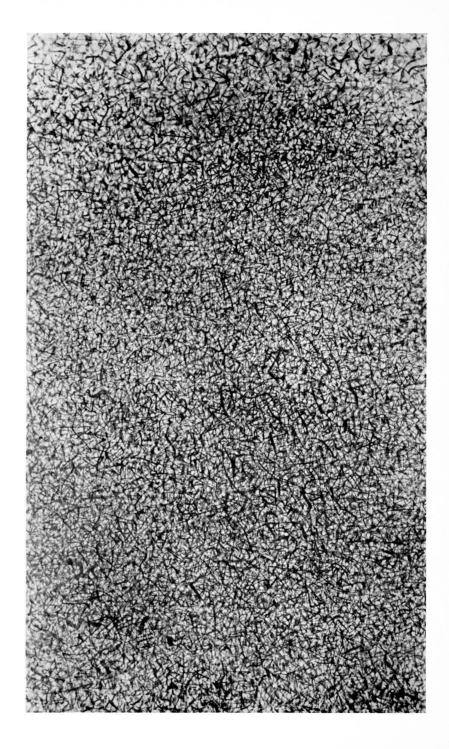

Plane of Poverty. 1960. Oil, 76¹/₄×45¹/₂″.
Collection Mr. and Mrs. Ira Haupt,
Asbury Park, New Jersey

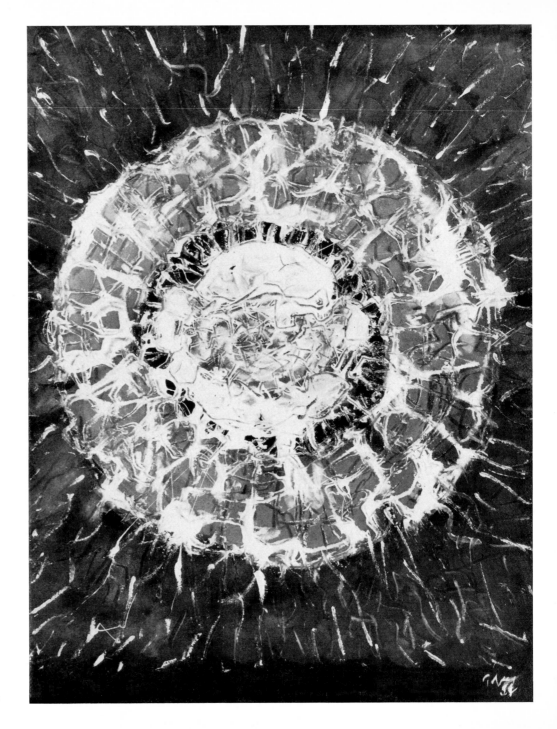

Space Rose. 1959. Tempera, 15³/4 × 11³/4″. Galerie Jeanne Bucher, Paris

1 For this statement by Tobey see Dorothy C. Miller, ed., *Fourteen Americans,* New York, The Museum of Modern Art, 1946, p. 70. All quotations separated from the text and printed in italics are from Mr. Tobey. Comments by him which are not footnoted come from a series of conversations, recorded on tape, between the painter and the author during the spring of 1962. Sources of other quotations are indicated in the usual manner. Certain of these have appeared in several places and versions; unfortunately it has not always been possible to determine the original instances.

On the idea of "roundness" in Tobey's painting, see Dore Ashton, "Mark Tobey et la rondeur parfaite," *XXe Siècle,* vol. 21, no. 12, May–June 1959, pp. 66–69. Miss Ashton points out references to roundness by Karl Jaspers, van Gogh, Joë Bousquet, and La Fontaine, which are cited by the French philosopher Gaston Bachelard in *La Poétique de l'espace,* Paris, 1958, p. 208.

2 Mark Tobey, "Reminiscence and Reverie," *Magazine of Art,* vol. 44, no. 6, Oct. 1951. This important article is abbreviated as *R & R* in subsequent notes.

3 The Bahá'í faith was the outcome of a religious movement in Persia led by a young man who, in 1844, took the name of the Báb (Gate). His teachings spread rapidly, but were declared heretical by the government and the Islamic clergy, who suppressed Bábism by force. In two decades more than 20,000 Bábís were martyred, often after torture, and the Báb was publicly shot in 1850.

Bahá'í was founded in 1863 by Mírzá Husayn 'Alí, a dedicated Bábí and the son of a government minister. In 1853, while in prison for Bábí activity, he became convinced that he was the prophet foretold by the Báb; when he announced his mission ten years later he took the title of Bahá'u'lláh (Glory of God). Most of the Bábís accepted his claim and became Bahá'ís (Followers of the Glory). Banished from Persia and Turkey, Bahá'u'lláh passed almost 40 years of his life imprisoned in the fortress city of 'Akká (Acre) in Palestine. There he composed the sacred scriptures, received visitors, and wrote many letters to heads of state urging world peace and other Bahá'í reforms. He died in 1892.

Bahá'u'lláh's will appointed his eldest son, 'Abdu'l-Bahá, as the interpreter of his teachings and exemplar of the faith, though not as a divine successor. After being freed by the Young Turks Revolution of 1908, 'Abdu'l-Bahá moved to Haifa. He traveled and lectured in Europe in 1911 and in the United States in 1912. He died in 1921, one year after being knighted by the British for humanitarian activities during World War I.

Bahá'í is now an expanding nonsectarian religion, active in more than 250 localities. Its shrines are the tombs of Bahá'u'lláh in 'Akká and 'Abdu'l-Bahá in Haifa, which is also the international center of Bahá'í. Its most important temple (begun in 1920 and dedicated in 1953) is in Wilmette, Illinois, near Chicago.

4 *The Faith of the Bahá'ís* (pamphlet), Wilmette, National Bahá'í Administrative Headquarters, n. d., p. 9.

5 *Ibid.,* p. 4.

6 *Bahá'í World Faith,* Wilmette, Bahá'í Publishing Trust, 1956, 2nd ed., p. 240.

7 *Ibid.,* p. 219.

8 *Ibid.,* pp. 224–225.

9 *Ibid.,* p. 228.

10 *Ibid.,* p. 229.

11 Exhibition catalogue, Willard Gallery, New York, 1949.

12 Catalogue, Exhibition of Contemporary American Painting, University of Illinois, Urbana, 1950, p. 211

13 For a comparison of Zen with Western philosophy and religion see William Barrett, "Zen for the West," in D. T. Suzuki, *Zen Buddhism,* Garden City, Doubleday, 1956, pp. vii-xx.

14 *Bahá'í World Faith,* p. 236.

15 *Ibid.,* p. 237.

16 "Mark Tobey Writes of his Painting on the Cover," *Art News,* vol. 44, no. 18, Jan. 1–14, 1946, p. 22.

17 Mark Tobey, comment in the files of the Willard Gallery.

18 *Bahá'í World Faith,* p. 170.

19 Mark Tobey, lecture at the Bahá'í Center, New York, Oct. 30, 1951. Tobey is quoting from Shoghi Effendi, a grandson of Bahá'u'lláh.

20 In *Art News,* vol. 56, no. 4, summer 1956, p. 39.

21 Mark Tobey, excerpts from a letter, *The Tiger's Eye,* no. 3, Mar. 15, 1948, p. 52.

22 *R & R,* p. 231.

23 Tobey quotes here from Bahá'u'lláh.

24 Mark Tobey, in a Bahá'í lecture, 1951 (see note 19).

25 Mark Tobey, *The Tiger's Eye,* p. 52 (see note 21).

26 B[elle] K[rasne], "A Tobey Profile," *The Art Digest,* vol. 26, no. 2, Oct. 15, 1951, pp. 26, 34.

27 Robert Motherwell and Ad Reinhardt, eds., *Modern Artists in America*, New York, Wittenborn-Schultz, 1951: "The Western Round Table on Modern Art" (1949), p. 30.

28 Denys Chevalier, "Une journée avec Mark Tobey," *Aujourd'hui*, vol. 6, no. 33, Oct. 1961, p. 7.

29 *R & R*, p. 232.

30 Among the masters of whom Tobey speaks with admiration are Michelangelo, Raphael, Titian, Bronzino, El Greco, Holbein, Grünewald (see note 82), Dürer, Rembrandt, Velazquez, Rubens, Guardi, Turner, Whistler, Monet, Cézanne, Inness, Liang K'ai, Mu-ch'i, Sesshu.

31 Krasne, *op. cit.*, p. 5.

32 Motherwell and Reinhardt, *op. cit.*, p. 28. The typescript of this session of "The Western Round Table on Modern Art" (in The Museum of Modern Art Library) contains an unedited version of this statement.

33 Mark Tobey, from a comment in the files of the Willard Gallery, New York, on the painting *Tundra* (1944).

34 Statement in the files of the Willard Gallery, Nov. 1942.

35 Mark Tobey, in *The Tiger's Eye*, p. 52 (see note 21).

36 Sidney Janis, *Abstract and Surrealist Art in America*, New York, Reynal and Hitchcock, 1944, p. 98.

37 Selden Rodman, *Conversations with Artists*, New York, Devin-Adair, 1957, p. 7.

38 On line as a means see Stanley William Hayter, "Line and Space of the Imagination," *View*, vol. 4, no. 4, pp. 126 ff., 140.

39 In *Search for the Real*, Andover, Addison Gallery of American Art, 1948, p. 71. It is interesting to note the complementary relationship of these two painters' ideas.

40 Mark Tobey, a comment on *Extensions from Bagdad* (1944) in the files of the Willard Gallery.

41 "As to the Sumi paintings – you ask how I came to do them . . . Offhand, I don't know really how I began this period – it happened one day, a suggestion from a brown-black painting which I felt could be carried on in blacks. How long I had these Sumi paintings in cold storage or had the delayed-unrealized desire to paint them I don't know. It was a kind of fever, like the earth in spring, or a hurricane. Of course I can give many reasons, that they were a natural growth from my experience with the brush and Sumi ink in Japan and China, but why did I wait some twenty years before doing them? There are so many suggestions on this question I could fill a book.

"Perhaps painting that way I freed myself or thought I did. Perhaps I wanted to paint without too much thought. I don't think I was in the Void, that rather popular place today. But then maybe I wanted to be – it's difficult to be faster than thought. Which screen of ourselves comes first – the inner when one wants to state an inner condition, knowing it has to take flesh to be understood and knowing also that, because of the outer covering, it will be side-tracked and sit there for eons understood as a symbol without reality? Already I have gone too far, but I feel I have kept the problem in view.

"How can I state in an understanding way why I did the Sumi paintings? Then, too, why after white writing should I turn to black ink? Well, the other side of the coin can be just as interesting, but to make myself simple I should remain a coin with only one side showing the imprint of man. It wouldn't be necessary to turn me over then – no need to order or compare. Ibsen expressed it very well when he said, 'Where I was ten years ago, you are now there but I am not with you.' " (Excerpt from a letter, Nov. 9, 1961. See Katharine Kuh, *The Artist's Voice*, New York, Harper & Row, 1962, pp. 244–245; two very important letters from Tobey included.)

42 *R & R*, p. 228.

43 Charles Rufus Morey, *Early Christian Art*, Princeton University Press, 1942, p. 7.

44 Chevalier, *op. cit.*, p. 9.

45 Comments on *Dormition of the Virgin* (1945) in the files of the Willard Gallery. An expanded version of this statement appeared in *Art News* in 1946 (see note 16).

46 In "The American Action Painters," *Art News*, vol. 51, no. 8, Dec. 1952, p. 49. Reprinted in his book *The Tradition of the New*, New York, Grove Press, 1961, p. 39. The advent of various forms of calligraphic brush and/or unfocused over-all treatment of form and space, and the relation between them in American painting during the forties and fifties, is a stylistic phenomenon demanding detailed study. It would draw in the entire ideology, aesthetics, and history of the New York School. Among the various influences felt by one or another of these painters and sculptors is the work of Masson, Miró, Mondrian, Kandinsky, and Soutine, and later that of Matta, Gorky, Pollock, and de Kooning; the idea of surrealist automatism, and later of Eastern calligraphy and Zen. The timetable by which painters (and sculptors) adopted these treatments is also of interest. In point of time, among American painters at least, Tobey was the first to unite calligraphy and post-cubist space, and it is known that his first exhibition as a mature artist, at the Willard Gallery in 1944, was received with interest and sympathy by de Kooning, Rothko, and other New York painters. However, the degree of his influence on Abstract Expressionism is difficult to determine, and to separate from its effect on painters who merely emulated his style. (On Tobey's critical reception in New York see

note 99.) Such a broad investigation of brush style and its meaning should be extended to include consideration of Hartung, Winter, Wols, Mathieu, Michaux, and other European artists, as well as recent Japanese abstract calligraphy.

47 *Broadway* and *Welcome Hero* are dated 1936, and *Broadway Norm* bears the date 1935 in two places. Tobey is positive that the three works were painted within a few nights of each other during the fall of 1935. Many of his early works were dated long after they were painted, so the possibility remains that the dates on *Broadway Norm* are in error, and that all three works were executed in 1936.

48 In an exhibition catalogue, Kootz Gallery, New York, 1951.

49 Excerpt from a letter, Oct. 28, 1954. See *The Art Institute of Chicago Quarterly*, vol. 49, no. 1, Feb. 1, 1955, p. 9. Also in Katharine Kuh, *The Artist's Voice*, pp. 240, 243, but in a revised form.

50 *R & R*, p. 230.

51 Rodman, *op. cit.*, p. 6.

52 Chevalier, *op. cit.*, p. 8.

53 From an undated letter. See "Textes de Tobey," *Rétrospective Mark Tobey*, Musée des Arts Décoratifs, Pavillon de Marsan, Paris, 1961, n. p.

54 Krasne, *op. cit.*, p. 34.

55 In 1960 Tobey worked on a large figure composition in oil, but abandoned it: "To weld the figure into space and keep it so you can see it," he concluded, "is almost impossible."

56 *R & R*, p. 231.

57 *R & R*, p. 230.

58 *Seattle Post Intelligencer*, Mar. 24, 1950.

59 Mark Tobey, comment on *Broadway Boogie* (also called *Emanations*) in the files of the Willard Gallery.

60 Excerpt from a letter to Marian Willard, Sept., 1946. See *Rétrospective Mark Tobey*, Musée des Arts Décoratifs, Pavillon de Marsan, Paris, 1961, n. p.

61 Excerpt from a letter, Oct. 28, 1954 (see note 49).

62 This comment has appeared in several slightly different versions; from the files of the Willard Gallery.

63 Mark Tobey, "Japanese Traditions and Modern Art," *College Art Journal*, vol. 18, no. 1, Fall 1958, p. 24.

64 Rodman, *op. cit.*, p. 17.

65 Krasne, *op. cit.*, p. 26.

66 *R & R*, p. 229.

67 Exhibition catalogue, Willard Gallery, New York, 1949.

68 For an analysis of the stages in the mystical ascent see Evelyn Underhill, *Mysticism*, New York, Meridian, 1955 (1st. ed. 1910), pp. 167 ff.

69 *R & R*, p. 230.

70 All Tobey's references to his childhood on pages 42 and 43 are from *R & R*, p. 230.

71 Mark Tobey, in a Bahá'í lecture, 1951 (see note 19).

72 Krasne, *op. cit.*, p. 5.

73 *R & R*, p. 232.

74 *Ibid.*, p. 231.

75 *Ibid.*

76 *Ibid.*

77 *Ibid.*

78 "The *Nude Descending the Staircase* looked to me like an explosion in a shingle mill, which I thought was the right kind of reasoning to settle it for all time. But later, after the blaze of Bellows and Henri, I saw it again in the painter's studio, thinking this time what a wonderful abstraction.

"Many times my ship has almost floundered, many times the sky has been too dark to know where art was going. The 1920's were enough to turn any creative heart into an organ without blood. Then I saw the 'Nude' again in Hollywood. It seemed full of the sorrows of the Son of Man. It's the Cruxifixion, I thought. I have never seen it since." (Excerpt from a statement in the catalogue of a Tobey exhibition: Portland Art Museum, San Francisco Museum of Art, Detroit Institute of Arts, 1945–1946.)

79 Excerpts from a letter, Oct. 23, 1954. See *The Art Institute of Chicago Quarterly*, vol. 49, no. 1, Feb. 1, 1955, p. 9.

80 From a letter, Oct. 28, 1954. See Kuh, *op. cit.*, p. 240.

81 Exhibition catalogue, California Palace of the Legion of Honor, 1951.

82 After visiting Grünewald's *Isenheim Altarpiece* in Colmar for the first time, Tobey recorded his intense impressions in a letter from Hindas, Sweden, to Charles and Ruth Seliger, dated Saturday, Aug. 29, 1954, from which an excerpt follows: "That day we went to Colmar, a really medieval town, and I saw at last the *great* Grünewald Altarpiece. I can't tell you how impressed I was. I really could have rewritten the story of the Cruxifixion on the spot. It showed only too clearly to me what a great universal idea married to a capable artist can become in the art world. The huge dark spaces of canvas became the devouring night, a universal gloom which sought to destroy all faith and hope. Mary Magdalene wringing her hands, all beautifully painted, on the point of her greatest despair. The mother in dramatic white – and what white and what a form – supported only by the long red arm of John. The Christ's body, mutilated to a state of horror, suggested all the Nazi camps one could imagine. His body growing heavier and heavier, all human life practically gone except in John the Baptist – serene and pointing, a witness

with a consciousness beyond human drama, a vision undisturbed which knows the light-dark spinning of the earth, and human drama is only a covering for the truth which is deathless."

Tobey's second visit to Colmar, several years later, was a disappointment. His overpowering response did not recur.

83 *R & R*, p. 230.

84 *Ibid.*

85 *Ibid.*, p. 229.

86 Mark Tobey, in *College Art Journal*, Fall, 1958, p. 21 (see note 63).

87 *R & R*, p. 229.

88 Tom Toomey, "Mark Tobey," *The Town Crier* (Seattle), Aug. 1, 1931, p. 7.

89 Muriel Draper, "Mark Tobey," *Creative Art*, vol. 7, no. 4, Oct., 1930, sup. p. 42.

90 Janet Flanner, "Tobey, mystique errant," *L'Oeil*, no. 6, June 15, 1955, p. 31.

91 *R & R*, p. 230.

92 In *College Art Journal*, Fall, 1958, p. 24 (see note 63).

93 *Ibid.*, p. 22.

94 Alexander Watt, "Paris Commentary," *The Studio*, vol. 162, no. 824, Dec., 1961, p. 223.

95 Watt, *op. cit.*, p. 224.

96 *Ibid.*

97 See note 47.

98 George Rowley, *Principles of Chinese Painting*, Princeton University Press, 1947, p. 4.

99 Tobey's introduction of calligraphy and Oriental painting into American abstract art must be seen as a peak in the history of an aesthetic *rapprochement* begun by the *chinoiserie* of the 18th century and carried forward by the impressionists through their painterly style and interest in Japanese prints. In the United States before the turn of the century, the American critic E. F. Fenollosa (one of the first to introduce Chinese and Japanese art to the West) realized that Oriental aesthetics could reform the academicism of American art teaching. Inspired by Fenollosa, these ideas were expanded and applied by Arthur Wesley Dow, at Pratt Institute, Columbia University, and at the Art Students League, and are explained in *Composition: A Series of Exercises in Art Structure for the Use of Students and Teachers*, first published in 1912 and now in its twentieth edition. Dow's greatest emphasis, however, was on "notans" – light-and-dark pattern – and his pedagogue's touch managed to deaden even the ink flinging of Sesshu.

The example of John Marin was of much greater importance, for it was practice rather than theory. With influ-

ences from impressionism, Cézanne, and cubism, Marin brilliantly preceded Tobey as a free-brush painter, and may even have looked at Oriental art or calligraphy. But whatever its antecedents, Tobey's fusion of East and West was surely the most specific, influential, and culturally significant America has seen.

Because of this, his international prominence since 1955, and his ambiguous relationship to the New York School, the "School of the Pacific," and *informel* painting in Europe, Tobey's critical reception in New York between his first show as a mature painter, in 1944, and the present, is of interest. It is an odd amalgam of lukewarm admiration, vacillating enthusiasm, and inattention. Although his exhibition at Romany Marie's in 1929 did not sell, pictures were chosen from it by Alfred H. Barr, Jr. for a group exhibition at The Museum of Modern Art. Reviewing the show in *The New Yorker*, Lewis Mumford wrote that he would not be surprised if the reputations of Tobey and Benjamin Kopman, though they worked "in symbols that are hard for the layman to swallow," would "survive their generation."

During the forties in Seattle, the press usually ridiculed Tobey's painting – "an air view of a week's washing still in the basket" – "the bottom of a child's cereal dish" – "the cracked bottom of a dried-up paint can" – but in New York Tobey's 1944 show was received with sympathy by both conservative and progressive critics. The catalogue included a perceptive foreword written by Sidney Janis, and Clement Greenberg, who was to play an influential role during the years to follow, wrote in *The Nation* (Apr. 22, 1944, p. 495) that, although Tobey's work was "not major," he had "already made one of the few original contributions to contemporary American painting." His unique style was described with understanding and precision: "Tobey's great innovation is his 'white writing': the calligraphic, tightly meshed interlacing of white lines which build up to a vertical, rectangular mass reaching almost to the edges of the frame; these cause the picture surface to vibrate in depth – or, better, toward the spectator. Yet this seems little out of which to compose an easel painting. The compensation lies in the intensity, subtlety, and directness with which Tobey registers and transmits emotion usually considered too tenuous to be made the matter of any other art than music." Three years later, in an article on American painting in the English publication *Horizon* (vol. 16, no. 93, Oct. 1947, p. 25), Greenberg wrote that, though they were influenced by Oriental art, and were "products of the Klee school," Morris Graves and Mark Tobey were "the two most original American painters today, in the sense of being the most uniquely and undifferentiatedly American." But then his emphasis shifted: ". . . since they have finished stating their personalities, Graves and Tobey have turned out to be so narrow as to cease even being interesting."

The forties and fifties in New York were not attuned to Tobey's quiet and contemplative art. Close in form (and sometimes in spirit) though Tobey was to the New York painters, the milieu was not his. Arresting, mural-size paintings were the new rule; small and meditative – let alone religious – themes were not favored. Yet (except for comments not worth remembering) Tobey was recognized, if only obliquely, as an important artist; he was ultimately dismissed by most avant-garde critics as decorative or "minor."

Thomas Hess's sensitive but oddly ambiguous comments in *Abstract Painting* (New York, Viking Press, 1951, p. 121) typify the New York response: "Without appealing to any common symbol or familiar shape, the artist invites us into a mystical contemplation of pure action – not for its sake alone, but to realize an almost religious duality of microscopic strength and giant frailty. But the beauty of *Structure* [one of the two paintings reproduced] is almost as minor as its parts, perfectly articulated though it and they may be.

The flaw here is, perhaps, not so much with Tobey as it is with the Oriental models to which he is so attached. Understatement to the point of preciosity and restraint to the degree where statement is innocuous – both flaws which so often mar Oriental painting – are evident in this modest tempera. Nonetheless, it points to a meeting place between the abstraction of paint and of idea – and this Wisconsin-born artist has been there many times."

Tobey has become internationally known during the last five years, and has surely not lacked attention. Therefore, it is surprising to discover that, in 1958, when he became the first American painter since Whistler (1895) to win a top prize at the Biennale of Venice, New York's two leading art magazines were not interested. *Arts* mentioned the historic event only in a news column, and *Art News* ignored it completely. *The New York Times* and *Life* printed feature articles. A similar lack of response followed Tobey's exhaustive retrospective at the Louvre (286 works listed) in 1961. To *Art News* it was worth a paragraph in a roundup of Paris exhibitions two months after it had closed; *Arts* later printed a poor review of the smaller version of the exhibition which traveled to London.

Tobey (seated) in fashion illustration studio, Chicago, c. 1910

left: Harrison Fisher signature. Detail from cover of *The Saturday Evening Post*, May 25, 1907. Picture Collection, New York Public Library

right: J. C. Leyendecker signature. Detail from cover of *The Saturday Evening Post*, Dec. 29, 1917. Picture Collection, New York Public Library

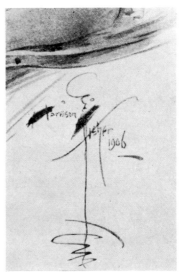

c. 1610   Henry Tobey emigrates from England to Massachusetts. (Tobey's lineage: British, Welsh, German, and Dutch.)

1890   December 11: Mark Tobey born in Centerville, Wisconsin, the youngest of four children of George Baker Tobey, a carpenter, housebuilder and farmer, and Emma Jane (Cleveland) Tobey.

1893   Family moves to land near Jacksonville, Tennessee. George Tobey builds a house, intending to start a sugarcane plantation. On discovering the lack of facilities for his children's education, decides to return north.

1894-   Family moves to Trempealeau, Wisconsin, a village of
1906   some 600 inhabitants on the Mississippi River. The Tobeys are devout Congregationalists, so Mark attends Sunday school and church regularly. In his free time he lives "the life of a barefoot boy," swimming, fishing, collecting wildflowers and specimens in the summer, and skating in the winter. He wants to be a minister, taxidermist, storekeeper, or trader. Tobey's mother refers to him as "the most restless young'un I ever had." No art was taught at the town school, but Mark was repeatedly chosen as blackboard illustrator, for other grades as well as his own. It was his father who led him toward art: one of Tobey's early memories is of a new pair of scissors, and of a desire to cut out the monkeys and other animals that his father drew in a "circular" style. George Tobey also carved animals from the red stone that the Indians of the region used for peace pipes. Jane Tobey was also creative: she made "wonderful rugs and things."

1906-   Family moves to Hammond, Indiana. Father buys son
1908   a pyrography outfit. Mark attends high school, where no art is taught except for an occasional session copying reproductions such as *Moonlight at Sea*. He is an excellent but erratic student, especially interested in subjects related to nature study, biology, and zoology. Tobey's brother Leon, his elder by ten years, learns the building trade and finally becomes a structural designer; but Mark, not drawn to his father's profession, resists the suggestion that he apprentice as a bricklayer. Father sends son to Chicago, twelve miles away, for Saturday classes at the Art Institute. He takes eight classes in watercolor with Frank Zimmerer, and two classes in oil with Professor Reynolds, who tells him that he has "the American handling bug." Because of his father's illness, Mark abandons high school after two years and seeks work.

1909-   Family moves to Chicago. Tobey finds work as a blue-
1911   print boy in the Northern Steel Works, where Leon is employed as a structural roof designer; takes a course in mechanical drawing. During his free time he pores over covers of *The Saturday Evening Post* and other popular magazines, hoping to become an illustrator. Fired from his job because he "didn't work hard enough," Tobey seeks work as a commercial artist. Hired as a shipping clerk by Barnes Crosby Engraving Co., a printing firm; the manager promotes him to the art department, where he is a failure as a letterer, and is fired along with his sponsor. After many difficulties in finding work he becomes an errand boy at $1.00 a week for an independent fashion studio run by a Mr. Moses who smokes Murad cigarettes incessantly. Tobey reveals a talent for drawing pretty girls' faces, and is assigned to adding faces for catalogue illustrations at $6.00 a week; raises in salary continue. By collecting clippings he gains an intimate knowledge of commercial illustrators, whose styles he can recognize by a single detail of brushwork. His favorites: Harrison Fisher, Howard Chandler Christy, Charles Dana Gibson, J. C. Leyendecker. He is convinced that "the American girl was the most beautiful thing you could set on canvas." Also admires Frederic Remington. A senior fashion artist throws some reproductions of Raphael, Rembrandt, and Michelangelo on Tobey's drawing table with the questions, "Why don't you paint something out of your own noodle? Why be a monkey?" During stolen time at the Art Institute, Tobey becomes acquainted with Italian Renaissance art, the painting of Zuloaga, and is impressed with the fluent brushwork of Sorolla, Sargent, and Hals. C. A. Schweitzer, an elderly Swiss from Basel, takes Tobey to German bookstores where he sees, in the magazines *Simplicissimus* and *Jugend*, the work of Franz von Lenbach, Franz von Stuck, Leo Putz, and other art nouveau artists.

1911   Takes the train to New York, determined to succeed as a fashion artist. Settles in Greenwich Village, 21 West 16th Street, below the philosopher and art critic Holger Cahill. Refused a job at *Pictorial Review*, but is hired by *McCall's* at $40.00 a week; later raised to $60.00.

1912   Returns to Chicago and continues work as a fashion artist, his salary going as high as $70.00 a week.

far left: *Self-Portrait.* (early 1920s).
Pastel, 24¹/₄ × 18¹/₄″. Collection
Mrs. Harold M. Hathaway, Seattle

left: *Portrait of Paul McCool.* 1925.
Conte crayon, 24 × 18¹/₄″. Collection
Mrs. Thomas D. Stimson, Seattle

below: Mark Tobey, Paris, 1925.
In background, two paintings by Tobey

1913   Sees the "Armory Show" at the Art Institute of Chicago, but the exhibition has little meaning for him. Duchamp's *Nude Descending a Staircase* resembles shingles (see note 78).

1913-   Travels back and forth between Chicago and New York.
1917   Discovers that he can make salable charcoal portraits, and thereby gains access to a fashionable circle.

1917   November: first one-man show, at M. Knoedler & Co., arranged by Marie Sterner. Among the subjects: Mary Garden (Tobey's patroness for a while), Muriel Draper, Jacques Copeau, Anthony Drexel Biddle, Juliet Thompson, and Governor Bell. At the instigation of Wymer Mills, an antique buyer for Wanamaker's who writes for *Vogue,* Tobey decorates the apartment of Edna Woolman Chase, its editor. Paints walls, lamps, screens, and "imitation tapestries." Abandons portraiture for interior decoration because it gives him more freedom. Takes two private lessons from Kenneth Hayes Miller for $7.00 each.

c. 1918   Meets a lady portrait painter and escorts her home on foot because he has no money. During the walk she asks Tobey to pose for her, and tells him that she is a follower of the Bahá'í World Faith. While posing at her studio he sees Bahá'í literature, and subsequently accepts an invitation to visit a Bahá'í camp in Maine, where he becomes a convert. At the Pierpont Morgan Library sees work by William Blake. Visits Marcel Duchamp.

1918 November 11: Tobey and Janet Flanner (later a well-known writer for *The New Yorker*) celebrate the armistice (see page 45).

1919- Reacts against the "Renaissance sense of space and or-
1920 der," and against sculptural form, moved by "a violent desire to break and disintegrate forms and to use light structures rather than dark." Paints *Descent into Forms*, now lost, and compositions "full of minute forms or patterns."

1920- Tobey remembers the twenties as a period of great con-
1922 fusion and brilliance. Draws caricatures, which become popular. *The Circle* by Somerset Maugham plays in New York and Tobey draws John Drew, Estelle Winwood, and others. Some are published in *The New York Times* — one of Lillian Gish "with her hand in her mouth."

1922- Does drawings of burlesque, vaudeville, Harlem dancers,
1923 and prostitutes. At the home of a girl who is a highly paid writer of scenarios for Hollywood, Tobey reads an account of a saying by St. Augustine, "We learn to do by doing." After an unsuccessful marriage, he decides to leave New York and apply this principle as a teacher of art. Goes to Seattle and finds a job in a progressive school of art, music, dance, and theater run by Miss Nellie Cornish, and is sponsored by Mrs. Edgar Ames. He is paid $2.00 a class from which the school takes $1.20, and begins teaching with four pupils. One evening at the Cornish School he makes what he now calls his "personal discovery of cubism" (see pages 45–47). Sees a few Japanese color prints.

1923- Meets Teng Kuei, a Chinese student at the University of
1924 Washington, who introduces Tobey to Chinese brushwork (see page 47).

1925 June: goes to Europe; settles in Paris on the rue de la Santé. Spends the winter at the home of his friends the Sanderses, in Châteaudun, near Chartres.

1926 January: travels with the Sanderses to Barcelona, Greece, Constantinople, and Beirut; makes a pilgrimage to the tombs of Bahá'u'lláh in 'Akká and 'Abdul-Bahá in Haifa. Intrigued by Persian and Arabic scripts. February: returns to Paris, living in the rue Visconti.

1927- Returns to Seattle, then divides his time between New
1929 York, Chicago, and Seattle. Carves some 100 pieces of soap sculpture, one of which is cast in brass by Howard Putzel, who is later to be influential in the New York avant-garde. During a visit in New York, Teng Kuei asks Tobey, as they look at a goldfish tank in a restaurant

Figure. c. 1928.
Brass sculpture, h. 3³/₄″.
Collection Mrs. Horton
C. Force, Seattle

window, why Western artists paint fish only when they are dead, and why Western paintings resemble holes in the wall. This further undermines Renaissance concepts in Tobey's eyes.

1929 December: one-man show at Romany Marie's Café Gallery (interior designed by Buckminster Fuller). Not a success, but A. H. Barr, Jr., sees it and selects pictures for the exhibition *Painting and Sculpture by Living Americans* at The Museum of Modern Art. Returns to Seattle where his teaching position at the Cornish School is threatened by the depression.

1930 Muriel Draper, mother of the dancer Paul Draper, writes the first major article on Tobey in *Creative Art*. Through the interest of Beatrice Straight, Mr. and Mrs. Leonard Elmhurst invite Tobey to teach (supposedly for six months) at Dartington Hall, their progressive school in Devonshire, England, in a picturesque setting some 200 miles from London.

1931 Trip to Mexico, where Tobey meets Martha Graham, Marsden Hartley, and René d'Harnoncourt.

1931- Tobey is resident artist at Dartington Hall. Among the
1938 many intellectuals and artists who teach or sojourn there during this period are Pearl Buck, Arthur Waley, Aldous Huxley, Rabindranath Tagore, Rudi Shankar and his dance company, and the Jooss ballet. Sees Turner's *The Burning of the Ships* at the Tate Gallery.

1932 Travels in Europe. Again visits Bahá'í shrines in Palestine.

c. 1933 Paints dry-fresco murals for the dance school at Dartington Hall.

1934 Granted leave for a study trip arranged by the Elmhursts, Tobey departs for the East with Bernard Leach, a painter and ceramist teaching at the school. They go to Colombo, Hong Kong, and Shanghai, where Tobey stays with Teng Kuei and his family; then, alone, he goes to Japan. Spends a month at a Zen monastery in Kyoto, studying calligraphy and painting, meditating, and writing poetry. Pen drawings done in England on wet paper are published in Japan. In June goes to San Francisco where he paints a series of "the animal world under moonlight" in a hotel room.

1935 November–December: first one-man museum exhibition, Seattle Art Museum. After a brief visit to Seattle returns to England via New York.

c. 1935 Back at Dartington Hall, Tobey paints *Broadway Norm, Broadway*, and *Welcome Hero* as a result of his Oriental experiences (see pages 48, 49 and note 47). These pictures synthesize Tobey's major discoveries and initiate the style later known as "white writing."

1937 Experiments with cubist still lifes.

1938 Leaves Dartington Hall for a short visit to New York, but world tension prevents his return to England; paints in a furnished room on 72nd Street. Goes to Seattle. Works for six months on the W. P. A. Federal Art Project. Begins teaching in his studio.

1939 Paints murals for the home of Mrs. John Baillargeon, now owned by Richard E. Fuller, Director of the Seattle Art Museum. The writer Nancy Wilson Ross introduces Tobey to Marian Willard, his future dealer in New York, who buys *Broadway*.

1940 In Seattle, during the 1940s, develops white writing, multiple space, moving focus, etc. Studies flute and piano. Wins Baker Memorial Award in Northwest Annual Exhibition, Seattle Art Museum, with *Modal Tide*, starting a local art controversy.

1942 Marian Willard enters *Broadway* in *Artists for Victory* exhibition at the Metropolitan Museum of Art in December. Wins a $500 purchase prize.

1943 Paints pictures based on three years of study in the Pike Place Public Market, Seattle.

1944 One-man exhibition at the Willard Gallery, New York. Beginning of national reputation.

left: Tobey's teaching studio at Dartington Hall.
right: Detail of Tobey's mural for the dance school, Dartington Hall, c. 1933.

Four Sketches, Pike Place Public Market, Seattle. 1941.
Watercolor and ink, $8^5/8 \times 5^5/8''$ each. Seattle Art Museum,
Eugene Fuller Memorial Collection

1945   November: wins fourth prize of $1000 in the 2nd annual *Portrait of America* exhibition at Rockefeller Center, New York.

1946   Included in Museum of Modern Art's *Fourteen Americans* exhibition.

1947   *Welcome Hero, Transition to Forms,* and three other works destroyed in a warehouse fire in Montana.

1948   Represented in the United States section at the XXIV Biennale of Venice.

1949   April 8–9: takes part in San Francisco Art Association's *Western Round Table on Modern Art.*

1950   Encouraged by Tobey, his friend Pehr Hallsten, a Swedish-American scholar, takes up painting, using his Christian name.

1951   April 19–21: participates in 26th Annual Convention of the Pacific Arts Association at the University of Washington. October: "Reminiscence and Reverie" published in *Magazine of Art.*

1952   Film, *Mark Tobey: Artist,* released by Orbit Films. Shown at film festivals in Venice and Edinburgh. Work shown in *American Vanguard* exhibition prepared by Sidney Janis, at Galerie de France, Paris.

1954   Fall: goes to Sweden to join Pehr. Elected to the National Arts Club. First one-man show at Otto Seligman Gallery. Seligman becomes Tobey's exclusive representative in Seattle.

1955   January: to Paris. Travels to England, Basel, and Bern for "Tendances Actuelles" exhibition at the Kunsthalle. Spends spring in Nice. April: one-man exhibition at the Galerie Jeanne Bucher, his first in Paris. Beginning of international reputation.

1956   Returns to Seattle. May: elected to National Institute of Arts and Letters. Awarded United States National Prize of $1000 in the Guggenheim International Award. Included in *American Artists Paint the City,* United States section at the XXVIII Venice Biennale.

1957   March–April: paints sumis (Japanese ink paintings) in Seattle. Awarded the American Institute of Architects Fine Arts Medal.

1958   Wins first prize of the Commune of Venice for painting at the XXIX Biennale. In July goes to Europe; to the World's Fair in Brussels; Italy and England (London, Devonshire, and Cornwall). Returns to New York in October. Fall issue of *College Art Journal* publishes his

"Japanese Traditions and American Art." Wins first *Art in America* award of $ 1000.

1959   During a brief stay in Seattle in April, is honored by a Seattle City Council Resolution of Civic Appreciation. Does a mural (8 × 9′) in the Washington State Library in Olympia (directly in oil on canvas) which, after a controversy, is dedicated on June 7 by Governor Rossellini. Summer: to Paris.

1960   Settles in Basel with Pehr and his secretary Mark Ritter. Paints new works to be shown in Louvre exhibition. Lives at 69 rue Saint Albanvorstadt until 1962. May 11: elected a member of the American Academy of Arts and Sciences, but fails to accept election. September: takes part in the Congress of the International Association of Plastic Arts, in Vienna, the subject of which is "Orient-Occident."

1961   October: Tobey Retrospective opens at the Musée des Arts Décoratifs, Paris (Palais du Louvre, Pavillon de Marsan). Wins first prize at the Carnegie Institute's *Pittsburgh International Exhibition of Contemporary Painting and Sculpture.*

1962   February: returns to New York with Pehr, and in March goes to Seattle. June: paints in Seattle studio.

Mark Tobey in his Seattle studio, 1962. In background, a work of sculpture by Claire Falkenstein.
Photograph: George Uchida

MAJOR EXHIBITIONS

ONE-MAN EXHIBITIONS

1917 M. Knoedler & Co., New York. Pencil portrait drawings, Nov. 17–24

1928 Arts Club of Chicago, Dec. 24–31

1929 Romany Marie's Café Gallery, New York. Dec. 2–31

1930 Cornish School, Seattle

1931 Contemporary Arts, New York. Mar.
Harry Hartman, Bookstore and Gallery, Seattle. Drawings and watercolors. Aug.

1934 Paul Elder Gallery, San Francisco
Beaux Arts Gallery, London. Feb. 6–24

1935 Stanley Rose Gallery, Hollywood
Seattle Art Museum, Nov.–Dec.

1940 Arts Club of Chicago

1942 Seattle Art Museum, Apr.–May

1944 Willard Gallery, New York. Apr. 4–29

1945 Portland Art Museum, Portland, Oregon. Jul. 7–Aug. 12. Shown thereafter at San Francisco Museum of Art, Sept. 8–30; Arts Club of Chicago, Feb. 7–27; Alger House, Detroit Institute of Arts, Mar., 1946
Willard Gallery, New York. Nov. 13–Dec. 8

1947 Willard Gallery, New York. Nov. 4–29

1949 Willard Gallery, New York. Nov. 1–26
Margaret Brown Gallery, Boston

1950 Willard Gallery, New York. Watercolors, Nov. 28–Dec. 30

1951 California Palace of the Legion of Honor, San Francisco. Mar. 31–May 6. Shown thereafter at Henry Gallery, Seattle (University of Washington), May 20–June 27; Santa Barbara Museum of Art, Aug. 16–Sept. 9; Whitney Museum of American Art, New York, Oct. 4–Nov. 4 (all slightly modified from original exhibition)
Margaret Brown Gallery, Boston. May 7–26
Willard Gallery, New York. Oct. 9–Nov. 3

1952 Renaissance Society, University of Chicago. Apr. 18–May 14
Zoe Dusanne Gallery, San Francisco

1953 Willard Gallery, New York. Apr. 1–May 2

1954 Margaret Brown Gallery, Boston. May 10–29
Willard Gallery, New York. Nov. 3–27
Otto Seligman Gallery, Seattle. Nov. 28–Dec. 3 (extended to Jan. 15, 1955)

1955 Art Institute of Chicago. Gallery of Art Interpretation. Jan. 21–Mar. 20
Gump's Gallery, San Francisco. Feb. 17–Mar. 15
Galerie Jeanne Bucher, Paris. Mar. 18–Apr. 9
Paul Kantor Gallery, Los Angeles. Apr. 25–May 20
Institute of Contemporary Arts, London. May 4–June 4 (exhibition from Paris)

1956 Margaret Brown Gallery, Boston. May 28–June 20

1957 Willard Gallery, New York. Sumi paintings, Nov. 12–Dec. 7
Otto Seligman Gallery, Seattle
Art Gallery of Greater Victoria, British Columbia

1958 Galerie Stadler, Paris. Jan. 17–21

1959 St. Albans School, Washington, D.C. May 21–June 3
Seattle Art Museum. Retrospective Exhibition, Sept. 11–Nov. 1. Shown thereafter at Portland Art Museum, Dec.–Jan. 1960; Colorado Springs Fine Arts Center, Jan.–Feb.; Pasadena Art Center, Feb.–Mar.; M. H. de Young Memorial Museum, San Francisco, Mar.–Apr.
Galerie Jeanne Bucher, Paris. Nov. 27–Jan. 16, 1960

1960 Fredric Hobbs Fine Art, San Francisco. Masterworks by Mark Tobey; First Public Exhibition of 16 Masterpieces on Loan from the Arthur and Joyce Dahl Collection, Sept. 12–Oct. 14
Kunsthalle, Mannheim. Dec. 17–Jan. 22, 1961

1961 Galerie Beyeler, Basel. May 15–June 30
Royal S. Marks Gallery, New York. Oct. 3–28
Musée des Arts Décoratifs, Paris (Palais du Louvre, Pavillon de Marsan). Oct. 18–Dec. 1

1962 The Whitechapel Art Gallery, London. Jan. 31–Mar. 4 (modified version of 1961 Paris exhibition)
Seattle World's Fair. Apr. 21–Oct. 21
Otto Seligman Gallery, Seattle. May 9–Jul. 31
The Phillips Collection, Washington, D.C. May 6–June 6 (extended to Jul. 6)

SELECTED GROUP EXHIBITIONS

1930 The Museum of Modern Art, New York. *Painting and Sculpture by Living Americans,* Dec. 2–Jan. 20, 1931

1931 Harvard Society for Contemporary Art, Cambridge, Mass. *Americans,* Feb. 21–Mar. 14

1939 New York World's Fair. *American Art Today*

1940 Art Institute of Chicago. *19th International Exhibition of Watercolors,* Apr. 25–May 26

1942 The Metropolitan Museum of Art, New York. *Artists for Victory,* Dec. 7–Feb. 22, 1943

1943 The Museum of Modern Art, New York. *Romantic Painting in America,* Nov. 17–Feb. 6, 1944

1944 Mortimer Brandt Gallery, New York. *Abstract and Surrealist Art in America,* Nov. 29–Dec. 30

The Metropolitan Museum of Art, New York. *1st Annual Portrait of America Exhibition,* sponsored by Pepsi-Cola Company, under the auspices of Artists for Victory, Inc.

1945 Brooklyn Museum, New York. *13th International Watercolor Exhibition,* Mar.–Apr.

Seattle Art Museum. *31st Annual Exhibition of Northwest Artists,* Oct. 3–Nov. 4

Rockefeller Center, New York. *2nd Annual Portrait of America Exhibition* (Pepsi-Cola), Nov.–Dec. (circulated to 8 cities in U.S.)

Whitney Museum of American Art, New York. *Annual Exhibition,* Nov. 27–Jan. 10, 1946

1946 Durand-Ruel Galleries, New York. *Modern Religious Paintings,* Jan. 9–Feb. 2

Whitney Museum of American Art, New York. *Annual Exhibition,* Feb. 5–Mar. 13

Colorado Springs Fine Arts Center. *8th Annual Exhibition of Paintings by Artists West of the Mississippi,* Mar.–Apr.

Virginia Museum of Fine Arts, Richmond. *Contemporary American Paintings* (5th Biennial Exhibition), Mar. 30–Apr. 25

Tate Gallery, London. *American Paintings from the 18th Century to the Present Day,* June–Jul.

Art Institute of Chicago. *57th Annual American Exhibition of Watercolors and Drawings,* June 6–Aug. 18

Colorado Springs Fine Arts Center. *New Accessions U.S.A.,* Jul. 15–Sept. 2

The Museum of Modern Art, New York. *Fourteen Americans,* Sept. 10–Dec. 8

Whitney Museum of American Art, New York. *Annual Exhibition,* Dec. 10–Jan. 16, 1947

1947 Colorado Springs Fine Arts Center. *9th Annual Exhibition of Paintings by Artists West of the Mississippi,* Mar. 4–Apr. 15

Munson-Williams-Proctor Institute, Utica, N.Y. *Ten Painters of the Pacific Northwest,* Oct. 1947; shown thereafter in Andover, Mass., Albany, N.Y., Buffalo, N.Y., and Baltimore, Maryland, to Mar. 1948

Art Institute of Chicago. *58th Annual American Exhibition of Watercolors and Drawings,* Nov. 6–Jan. 11, 1948

California Palace of the Legion of Honor, San Francisco. *2nd Annual Exhibition of Painting,* Nov. 19–Jan. 4, 1948

Whitney Museum of American Art, New York. *Annual Exhibition,* Dec. 6–Jan. 25, 1948

1948 Rotunda Gallery, San Francisco. *Tobey, Anderson, Callahan . . .,* Jan. 6–31

Colorado Springs Fine Arts Center. *10th Annual Exhibition of Paintings by Artists West of the Mississippi,* Feb. 25–Apr. 11

Venice, XXIV Biennale. *U.S. Representation,* Jul. 14–Sept. 14

The Museum of Modern Art, New York. *New York Private Collections,* Jul. 20–Sept. 12

Art Institute of Chicago. *59th Annual American Exhibition of Watercolors and Drawings,* Nov. 4–Jan. 2, 1949

California Palace of the Legion of Honor, San Francisco. *3rd Annual Exhibition of Painting,* Dec. 1–Jan. 16, 1949

1949 Colorado Springs Fine Arts Center. *11th Annual Exhibition of Paintings by Artists West of the Mississippi,* Feb. 8–Mar. 28

University of Illinois, Urbana. *Exhibition of Contemporary American Painting.* Feb. 27–April 3

Whitney Museum of American Art, New York. *Annual Exhibition,* Apr. 2–May 8

San Francisco Museum of Art. *Special Exhibition in conjunction with the Western Round Table on Modern Art,* Apr.

Samuel M. Kootz Gallery, New York. *The Intrasubjectives,* Sept. 14–Oct. 3

The Art Gallery of Toronto. *Contemporary Paintings from Great Britain, the U.S. and France,* Nov.–Dec.

Whitney Museum of American Art, New York. *Annual Exhibition,* Dec. 16–Feb. 5, 1950

1950 University of Illinois, Urbana. *Exhibition of Contemporary American Painting,* Feb. 26–Apr. 2

The Society of the Four Arts, Palm Beach. *From the Armory Show to the Present,* Mar. 9–31

Virginia Museum of Fine Arts, Richmond. *American Painting 1950,* Apr. 22–June 4

Seattle Art Museum. *36th Annual Exhibition of Northwest Artists,* Oct. 4–Nov. 5

Walker Art Center, Minneapolis. *Contemporary American Painting,* Oct. 15–Dec. 10

The Metropolitan Museum of Art, New York. *American Painting Today,* Dec. 8–Feb. 25, 1951

California Palace of the Legion of Honor, San Francisco. *4th Annual Exhibition of Contemporary American Painting,* Nov. 25–Jan. 1, 1951
Portland (Oregon) Art Museum. *Callahan, Tobey and Graves,* Dec.

1951 The Museum of Modern Art, New York. *Abstract Painting and Sculpture in America.* Jan. 23–Mar. 25
Ueno Art Gallery, Tokyo. *Tokyo Independent Art Exhibition,* Feb. 27–Mar. 18 (circulated to 8 Japanese cities)
University of Illinois, Urbana. *Exhibition of Contemporary American Painting,* Mar. 4–Apr. 15
Whitney Museum of American Art, New York. *Annual Exhibition,* Mar. 17–May 6
Brooklyn Museum, New York. *16th International Watercolor Exhibition,* May-June
University Gallery, University of Minnesota, Minneapolis. *40 American Painters, 1940–1950,* June 4–Aug. 30
University of Colorado, Boulder. *Exhibition of Paintings,* June 6–Aug. 15
University of Wisconsin, Madison. *Significant American Painting,* summer
Rathaus Schöneberg, Berlin. *Amerikanische Malerei Werden und Gegenwart,* Sept. 20–Oct. 5; shown thereafter at Schloss Charlottenburg, Berlin, Oct. 10–24
São Paulo. I Bienal, Museu de Arte Moderna, *U. S. Representation.* Oct.–Dec.
Seattle Art Museum. *37th Annual Exhibition of Northwest Artists,* Oct. 3–Nov. 4
Art Institute of Chicago. *60th Annual American Exhibition,* Oct. 25–Dec. 16
City Art Museum of St. Louis. *Contemporary American Painting,* Nov. 12–Dec. 10
Brooklyn Museum, New York. *Revolution and Tradition,* Nov. 15–Jan. 6, 1952
Sidney Janis Gallery, New York. *American Vanguard for Paris;* shown at Galerie de France, Paris, 1952

1952 Wildenstein Galleries, New York. *Twentieth-Century American Paintings,* Feb. 29–Mar. 22
Whitney Museum of American Art, New York. *Annual Exhibition,* Mar. 13–May 4
Rose Fried Gallery, New York. *10 American Abstract Painters.* Mar. 24–Apr. 11
City Art Museum of St. Louis. *St. Louis Collects,* Apr. 7–May 5
Colorado Springs Fine Arts Center. *New Accessions U. S. A.,* Jul. 3–Sept. 2

Museum of Cranbrook Academy of Art, Bloomfield Hills, Mich. *Light and the Painter,* Sept. 5–29
Seattle Art Museum. *38th Annual Exhibition of Northwest Artists,* Oct. 8–Nov. 2
Pittsburgh International Exhibition of Contemporary Painting, Carnegie Institute, Oct. 16–Dec. 14
Whitney Museum of American Art, New York. *Annual Exhibition,* Nov. 6–Jan. 4, 1953
Union Theological Seminary, New York. *Exhibition of Contemporary Religious Art,* Dec. 1–16

1953 Contemporary Art Association of Houston, Texas. *Modern Painting, Ways and Means,* Jan. 25–Feb. 15
Colorado Springs Fine Arts Center. *14th Annual Exhibition of Paintings by Artists West of the Mississippi,* Mar. 8–Apr. 28
Whitney Museum of American Art, New York. *Annual Exhibition,* Apr. 9–May 29
Seattle Art Museum. *39th Annual Exhibition of Northwest Artists,* Oct. 7–Nov. 8
2nd International Art Exhibition, Japan, 7 cities, 1953; and Honolulu, 1954. *U. S. Representation – Seven American Watercolorists*

1954 Sidney Janis Gallery, New York. *9 Americans,* Jan. 4–30
Galerie Rive Droite, Paris. *Signes Autres,* Jan. 18–Feb. 8
Virginia Museum of Fine Arts, Richmond. *American Painting 1954,* Feb. 26–Mar. 21; shown at Des Moines (Iowa) Art Center, Apr. 4–May 2
Whitney Museum of American Art, New York. *Annual Exhibition,* Mar. 17–Apr. 18
Contemporary Arts. Inc., New York. *High Spots 1929–1940,* May 10–28
Margaret Brown Gallery, Boston. *Mark Tobey, Morris Graves,* May 10–29
Galleria dello Spazio, Rome. *Caratteri della Pittura d'Oggi,* June
Pavillon Vendôme, Aix-en-Provence. *Le Dessin contemporain aux Etats-Unis,* Sept.; shown at the Musée National d'Art Moderne, Paris, Oct.–Nov.
Art Institute of Chicago. *61st American Exhibition,* Oct. 21–Dec. 5

1955 Whitney Museum of American Art, New York. *Annual Exhibition,* Jan. 12–Feb. 20
Kunsthalle, Bern. *Tendances Actuelles,* Jan. 29–March 6
University of Illinois, Urbana. *Exhibition of Contemporary American Painting.* Feb.–Apr.
3rd International Art Exhibition, Japan, 8 cities. *U. S. Representation*

Musée National d'Art Moderne, Paris. *50 ans d'art aux Etats-Unis*, Selections from the Collections of The Museum of Modern Art, New York, Mar. 30–May 15; shown thereafter in Zurich, Frankfurt, Barcelona (for the III Bienal Hispanoamerica, Hispanoamericana de arte, Sept. 24–Oct. 24), London, The Hague, Vienna, Belgrade, 1955–1956

São Paulo. III Bienal, Museu de Arte Moderna, *U. S. Representation,* June–Oct.

Galerie Stadler, Paris. *Group Exhibition,* Oct.–Nov.

Pittsburgh International Exhibition of Contemporary Painting. Carnegie Institute, Oct. 13–Dec. 18

Wadsworth Atheneum, Hartford, Conn. *20th-Century Painting from Three Cities,* Oct. 19–Dec. 4

Seattle Art Museum. *41st Annual Exhibition of Northwest Artists,* Nov. 9–Dec. 4

Whitney Museum of American Art, New York. *Annual Exhibition,* Nov. 9–Jan. 8, 1956

1956 Galerie d'Art Moderne, Basel. *Group exhibition, Mannessier, Singier, Poliakoff, Tobey, Vieira da Silva,* Jan.–Feb.

Kunsthalle, Basel. *Japanische Kalligraphie und Westliche Zeichen,* Feb. 18–Mar. 18

Exposition Internationale de l'Art Actuel. Japan, 3 cities

Contemporary Arts Museum of Houston. *Contemporary Calligraphers – Marin, Tobey, Graves,* Apr. 12–May 13

Whitney Museum of American Art, New York. *Annual Exhibition,* Apr. 18–June 10

Yale University Art Gallery, New Haven. *Pictures Collected by Yale Alumni,* May 8–June 18

American Academy of Arts and Letters, New York. *Exhibition of Works by Newly Elected Members* (of the National Institute of Arts and Letters), May 24–June 24

Venice. XXVIII Biennale, *U. S. Representation, American Artists Paint the City,* June 16–Oct. 21

Galerie Stadler, Paris. *Structures en devenir,* Oct. 16–Nov. 15

Rose Fried Gallery, New York. *Modern Masters,* Oct. 22–Nov. 30

Seattle Art Museum. *42nd Annual Exhibition of Northwest Artists,* Nov. 8–Dec. 2

Whitney Museum of American Art, New York. *Annual Exhibition,* Nov. 14–Jan. 6, 1957

Darmstadt, Lille, Marseilles, Paris, Tours, Toulouse, Rouen. *Contemporary American Painters,* 1956–57

1957 Renaissance Society, University of Chicago. *Contemporary American Watercolors,* Feb. 17–Mar. 15

New Delhi, India. *3rd International Contemporary Art Exhibition,* Feb. 23–Mar. 7; shown in 6 Indian cities

Colorado Springs Fine Arts Center. *16th Annual Exhibition of Paintings by Artists West of the Mississippi,* Apr. 3–June 30

Munson-Williams-Proctor Institute, Utica. N. Y. *1884–1956, An American Collector – Edward Wales Root,* Apr. 28–May 26

Minneapolis Institute of Arts. *American Paintings: 1945-1957,* June 18–Sept. 1

Museum of Art, Ogunquit, Maine. *Pacific Northwest Painters and Sculptors,* June 29–Sept. 9

Whitney Museum of American Art, New York. *Annual Exhibition,* Nov. 20–Jan. 12, 1958

Eight American Artists. Exhibition organized by the USIA for Europe and Asia; shown in Copenhagen, Frankfurt, Berlin, Nuremberg, Munich, Hamburg, Essen, London, York, Bordeaux, Paris, Saint-Etienne; Seoul, Taegu, Tokyo, Kobe, Kyoto, Magoya, Matsuyama, Hiroshima, Osaka, Sapporo, Manila, Wellington, Auckland, Melbourne, Sidney, 1957–58 (shown at Seattle Art Museum, 1957)

1958 Montreal Museum of Fine Arts. *Contemporary American Painters,* Jan. 7–26

Whitney Museum of American Art, New York. *Nature in Abstraction,* Jan. 14–Mar. 16 (shown in 6 American cities, 1958–59)

Galerie des Beaux-Arts, Bordeaux. *Peinture de l'ouest, sculpture de l'est des Etats-Unis,* Feb. 7–19; also shown at Musée de Saint-Etienne, Apr. 24–June 1

Palais des Beaux-Arts, Brussels. *50 ans d'art moderne,* Apr. 17–Oct. 19

Whitney Museum of American Art, New York. *The Museum and Its Friends,* Apr. 30–June 15

Des Moines Art Center. *10th Anniversary Exhibition; Current Painting Styles and Their Sources,* June 1–Jul. 20

Detroit Institute of Arts, and Lawrence Fleischman Collection. *9 Generations of American Painting* (circulated by USIA to 4 cities in Israel, beginning with Bezalel National Museum, Jerusalem, June

Venice. XXIX Biennale. *U. S. Representation, Lipton, Rothko, Smith, Tobey* (35 works), June 14–Oct. 19

Munson-Williams-Proctor Institute, Utica. *American Paintings and Drawings from the Edward W. Root Bequest,* Aug.

University of St. Thomas, Houston, Texas. *Islands Beyond,* Oct. 2–19

Venice. *Exhibition of Prize-Winning Paintings and Sculptures at the Venice Biennale,* Nov.

Seattle Art Museum. *44th Annual Exhibition of Northwest Artists,* Nov. 6–Dec. 7

Museum of Fine Arts of Houston. *A Decade of Contemporary American Drawings,* Nov.–Dec.

Whitney Museum of American Art, New York. *Annual Exhibition,* Nov. 19–Jan. 4, 1959

Musée Cernuschi, Paris. *Orient-Occident: rencontres et influences durant cinquante siècles d'art,* Nov.–Feb. 1959

Pittsburgh International Bicentennial Exhibition of Contemporary Painting and Sculpture. Carnegie Institute, Dec. 6–Feb. 8, 1959

1959 *Modern American Painting.* Exhibition organized by the USIA and shown at the Kunstmuseum, St. Gallen, Switzerland; Hessisches Landesmuseum, Darmstadt, Germany; Göteborg Konstmuseum (Sweden), 1959–61

Whitney Museum of American Art, New York. *The Museum and Its Friends,* Mar. 5–Apr. 12

University of Illinois, Urbana. *Contemporary American Painting and Sculpture,* Mar.–Apr.

Whitney Museum of American Art, New York. *The Collection of the Sara Roby Foundation,* Apr. 29–June 14

Circolo degli Artisti, Turin. *Arte nuova; Esposizione internazionale di pittura e scultura,* May 6–June 15

Portland (Oregon) Art Museum. *Paintings and Sculptures of the Pacific Northwest,* June 13–Aug. 9

Kassel, Germany. *Documenta II,* Jul. 11–Oct. 11

Moscow. *American National Exhibition,* Jul. 25–Sept. 5

City Art Museum of St. Louis. *Twenty-Five Years of American Painting,* Sept.–Oct. (circulated by USIA to 8 European cities, Nov. 1959–Sept. 1960

Whitney Museum of American Art, New York. *Paintings and Sculpture from the American National Exhibition in Moscow,* Oct. 28–Nov. 15

The Dallas Museum for Contemporary Arts. *Signposts of 20th Century Art,* Oct. 28–Dec. 7

Art Institute of Chicago. *63rd American Exhibition,* Dec. 2–Jan. 31, 1960

Whitney Museum of American Art, New York. *Annual Exhibition,* Dec. 9–Jan. 31, 1960

1960 Columbus (S. C.) Gallery of Fine Art, *Contemporary American Painting,* Jan. 14–Feb. 18

The Museum of Modern Art, New York. *Art Lending Service Retrospective, 1950–1960,* Jan. 26–Mar. 20

Musée des Arts Décoratifs, Paris. *Antagonismes,* Feb.

University of California, Berkeley. *Art from Ingres to Pollock,* Mar. 6–Apr. 3

Whitney Museum of American Art, New York. *Business Buys American Art,* Mar. 17–Apr. 24

Walker Art Center, Minneapolis. *60 American Painters, 1960.* Apr.–May

Galerie Jeanne Bucher, Paris. *Hommage à Jeanne Bucher 1925–1960,* May 6–June 30

Yale University Art Gallery, New Haven. *Paintings, Drawings and Sculpture Collected by Yale Alumni,* May 19–June 26

M. Knoedler & Co., Inc., New York. *American Art 1910–1960; Selections from the Collection of Mr. and Mrs. Roy R. Neuberger,* June 8–Sept. 9

Esther Stuttman Gallery, New York. *The Current Scene, American Painting,* Nov. 8–Dec. 3

Whitney Museum of American Art, New York. *Annual Exhibition, Sculpture and Drawing,* Dec. 7–Jan. 22, 1961

1961 Art Institute of Chicago. *64th American Exhibition,* Jan. 6–Feb. 5

Palais des Beaux-Arts, Brussels. *Collection de M. et Mme William A. M. Burden,* Feb. 27–Mar. 15

Kunstmuseum, Düsseldorf. *Malerei seit 1945 aus der Sammlung Dotremont,* Mar.; shown at Kunsthalle, Basel, Apr. 22–May 28

Galleria Civica d'Arte Moderna, Turin. *La Pittura Moderna Straniera nelle Collezioni Private Italiane,* Mar.–Apr.

The Solomon R. Guggenheim Museum, New York. *100 Paintings from the G. David Thompson Collection,* May 25–Aug. 27. Shown previously at the Kunsthaus, Zurich, Oct.–Nov. 1960; Kunstmuseum, Düsseldorf, Dec. 14, 1960–Jan. 21, 1961; Gemeentemuseum, The Hague, Feb. 17–Apr. 9, 1961)

Milwaukee Art Institute. *10 Americans,* Oct.

Whitney Museum of American Art, New York. *30th Anniversary Exhibition; American Art of This Century,* Nov. 15–Dec. 10

Pittsburgh International Exhibition of Contemporary Painting and Sculpture. Carnegie Institute, Oct. 27–Jan. 7, 1962

Whitney Museum of American Art, New York. *Annual Exhibition; Contemporary American Painting,* Dec. 13–Feb. 4, 1962

1962 Seattle World's Fair. *Art Since 1950.* Apr. 21–Oct. 21

Ca'Pesaro, Venice. *Exhibition of Work by Grand Prize Winners at Venice Biennale, 1948–1960.* June 16–Oct. 7

SELECTED BIBLIOGRAPHY   by Inga Forslund, *Reference Librarian*

TEXTS BY TOBEY *(arranged chronologically)*

1 Beyond Chihuahua. *The Town Crier* (Seattle) Sept. 17, 1932.

2 Art and community. *World Order* v. 5 no. 1 : 33–34 April 1939.

3 "Artists' mind at work." *Limited Edition* Dec. 1945.
    Statement by Tobey.

3ª [Statement.] *In* "Fourteen Americans." Museum of Modern Art, 1946, p. 70. See bibl. 195.

4 "Mark Tobey writes of his painting on the cover" [Dormition of the Virgin.] *Art News* v. 44 no. 18: 22 Jan. 1–14, 1946.

5 [Excerpts from a letter.] *The Tiger's Eye* no. 3 : 52–57 incl. ill. Mar. 15, 1948.

6 [Statement.] *In* "Mark Tobey." N.Y., Willard Gallery, Nov. 1–26, 1949. p. [3].

7 [Statements.] *In* "Modern artists in America." Ed. by Robert Motherwell, Ad Reinhardt. N. Y., Wittenborn Schultz, 1951. Ser. 1, p. 27 ff*, 145.
    * Reprint from San Francisco panel "The western round table on modern art (1949)."

8 [Statements.] *In* "Retrospective exhibition of paintings by Mark Tobey." San Francisco, California Palace of the Legion of Honor, Mar. 31 – May 6, 1951. p. [4].

9 "Reminiscence and reverie." *Magazine of Art* v. 44 no. 6: 228–232 incl. ill. Oct. 1951.
    See also bibl. 204.

10 [Statements.] *In* "Mark Tobey: retrospective exhibition." N.Y., Whitney Museum of American Art, Oct. 4 – Nov. 4, 1951. p. [4–7].

11 [Statements.] *In* "Premier bilan de l'art actuel 1937–1953," éd. par Robert Lebel. Paris, 1953. p. 323.

12 [Statement.] *In* "Mystic painters of the Northwest." *Life* v. 35 no. 13: 84 Sep. 28, 1953.

13 Lyonel Feininger. *In* "Lyonel Feininger: recent paintings and watercolors (1951–1954)." N.Y. Curt Valentin Gallery, Mar. 30–Apr. 24, 1954. p. [3].

14 [Introduction to:] June Nye-Fay Chong exhibition. Otto Seligman Gallery, Seattle, Apr. 7–May 2, [1954?]

15 [Introduction to:] Georges A. Mathieu. Galerie Rive Droite, Paris, Nov. 5–30, 1954.

16 [Excerpts from a letter.] *Art Institute of Chicago Quarterly* v. 49 no. 1: 9 Feb. 1, 1955.
    Excerpts from a letter written by Mark Tobey, Oct. 28, 1954, from Paris in connection with a small retrospective exhibition of his work.

17 [Statements.] *In* "Contemporary calligraphers: John Marin, Mark Tobey, Morris Graves." Houston, Contemporary Arts Museum, Apr. 12–May 13, 1956.

18 [Statement.] *In* "New art in America." Ed. by John I. H. Baur. Greenwich, Conn., New York Graphic Society, 1957. p. 194.

19 Japanese traditions and American art. *College Art Journal* v. 18 no. 1: 20–24 Fall 1958.
    Also in *Arts Review* v. 14 no. 3: 12, 16 Feb. 24, 1962. – Based on a paper read at the Sixth National Conference of the United States Commission for Unesco held at San Francisco in November 1957. – Copy of typescript in Museum of Modern Art Library.

20 Introduction to: "Music to be seen." A portfolio of drawings by Ulfert Wilke. Louisville, Kentucky, Erewhon press [1959]. Limited edition of 350 copies.

21 [Statement.] *In* "Signposts of twentieth century art." Dallas, Museum for Contemporary Arts, Oct. 28–Dec. 7, 1959. p. 53.

22 [Statements.] *In* "Honest prophet." *Time* v. 74 no. 24 Dec. 14, 1959.

23 [Introduction to:] Nina Jacobson exhibition. Bodley Gallery, New York, Apr. 4–16, 1960.

24 KUH, KATHARINE. The painter meets the critic. *Saturday Review* v. 43 no. 27: 31–32 July 2, 1960.
    Interview with Tobey.

25 INTERNATIONAL ASSOCIATION OF PLASTIC ARTS. [Meeting: Artists from Eastern and Western countries.] 1960.
    Mimeographed minutes of meetings, held in Vienna Sept. 24–Sept. 28, 1960. – Tobey represented United States.

26 [Introduction to:] Pehr exhibition. Galerie Jeanne Bucher, Paris, Jan. 18, 1961.

27 [Statements.] *In* "Mark Tobey." Basel, Galerie Beyeler, May–June, 1961.

28 CHEVALIER, DENYS. Une journée avec Mark Tobey. *Aujourd'hui* 6 no. 33: 4–13 ill. Oct. 1961.
    Interview. – Includes also "Opinions sur Mark Tobey" p. 10–12.
    Also (in German) in *Das Kunstwerk* v. 15 no. 5/6: 44–49 ill. Nov.–Dec. 1961.

29 LEMONNIER, PIERRE. Qui est Mark Tobey? *Le Figaro littéraire* Oct. 14, 1961.

30 LEWINO, WALTER. Rencontre avec Marc Tobey, père de l'École du Pacifique. *Combat* Oct. 18, 1961.

31 Search without end. *Newsweek* Nov. 6, 1961.

32 CHEVALIER, DENYS. Un entretien avec Mark Tobey. *Pour l'Art* 81:33–37, 39 incl. ill. Nov.–Dec. 1961.
　　Interview.

33 [Statements.] *In* "Paris commentary" by Alexander Watt. *The Studio* v. 162 no. 824:223–224, 235 Dec. 1961.

34 CHEVALIER, DENYS. Tobey et les dangers de l'espace. Propos recueillis par Denys Chevalier. *XXe Siècle* n. s. 24 no. 18 suppl. (Chroniques du jour) 2p. incl. ports., Feb. 1962.
　　Interview.

35 KUH, KATHARINE. The artist's voice. p. 240–248.
　　To be published by Harper & Row, N.Y., in Oct. 1962. Contains interview with Tobey and letters from him.

　　For supplementary statements, quotations, brief extracts etc. see also bibl. 56, 194, 195, 207, 209.

MONOGRAPHS

36 CHOAY, FRANÇOISE. Mark Tobey. Paris, Hazan, 1961. [12] p. plus 12 col. pl. (Peintres d'aujourd'hui).

37 ROBERTS, COLETTE. Tobey. Paris, Le Musée de Poche, 1959. 46p. plus ill. (col. pl.) (Collection Le Musée de Poche.)
　　Also English edition, New York, Grove Press, 1960. (Evergreen Gallery Books. no. 4.)

GENERAL WORKS

38 Art since 1945. N.Y., Abrams, 1958. p. 293, col. pl. 145, pl. 160.

39 BARR, ALFRED H., Masters of modern art. N.Y., Museum of Modern Art, 1954. p. 174 incl. ill.

40 BAUR, JOHN I.H., ed. New art in America. Greenwich, Conn., New York Graphic Society, 1957. p. 193–197 incl. ill. (Mark Tobey by Dorothy C. Miller.)
　　Statement by Tobey p. 194.

41 BAUR, JOHN I. H. Revolution and tradition in modern American art. Cambridge, Mass., Harvard Univ. Press, 1951. p. 118, ill. 196.
　　Also Italian edition: "Le arti figurative in America 1900–1950." Rome, Edizioni di Storia e Letteratura, 1954. p. 166–168, pl. 196.

42 BAYL, FRIEDRICH. Bilder unserer Tage. Cologne, DuMont Schauberg, 1960. p. 97, col. pl. p. 32.
　　Text from Museum of Modern Art exhibition catalogue "Fourteen Americans." 1946.

43 BLESH, RUDI. Modern art U.S.A. Men, rebellion, conquest, 1900–1956. N.Y., Knopf, 1956. p. 262–264 and passim.

44 BRION, MARCEL. Art abstrait. Paris, Albin Michel, 1956. p. 294.

45 CASSOU, JEAN. Panorama des arts plastiques contemporains. Paris, Gallimard, 1960. p. 528, 531, 532, 536, 702.

46 CERNI, VICENTE AGUILERA. Arte norteamericano del siglo XX. Valencia, Fomento de Cultura, 1957. p. 116, pl. 106.

47 CIRLOT, JUAN-EDUARDO. Arte contemporáneo. Barcelona, E.D.H.A.S.A., 1958. p. 162, pl. 153.

48 CIRLOT, JUAN EDUARDO. El arte otro. Barcelona, Seix Barral, 1957. p. 66–71 (Mark Tobey y sus "Escrituras blancas.")

49 CIRLOT, JUAN EDUARDO. Informalismo. Barcelona, Omega, 1959. p. 32–34 ("Estados Unidos. Mark Tobey y otros"), ill. p. 64.

50 Les Clés de l'art moderne. Paris, La Table Ronde, 1955. p. 236–237.

51 GOODRICH, LLOYD, & BAUR, JOHN I. H. American art of our century. N.Y., Praeger, 1961. p. 208, 209 (ill.), 216.

52 GREENBERG, CLEMENT. Art and culture. Boston, Beacon Press, 1961. p. 217–218 (of chapter: "American type painting.")
　　Tobey also mentioned p. 156.

53 HESS, THOMAS B. Abstract painting: background and American phase. N.Y., Viking Press, 1951.

54 HITCHCOCK, HENRY-RUSSELL. Painting toward architecture. N.Y., Duell, Sloan & Pearce, 1948. p. 98, pl. p. 99.
　　The Miller Company collection of abstract art.

55 HUNTER, SAM. Modern American painting and sculpture. N.Y., Dell, 1959. p. 123–124, 218–219, pl. 23.

56 JANIS, SIDNEY. Abstract & surrealist art in America. N.Y., Reynal & Hitchcock, 1944. p. 87, 98–99 (ill.).
　　Brief statement by Tobey p. 98.

57 LANGUI, EMILE. 50 years of modern art. N.Y., Praeger, 1959. p. 331, ill. p. 220.
　　Originally catalogue of exhibition *50 ans d'art moderne*, Brussels, Palais des Beaux-Arts, 1958.

58 LARKIN, OLIVER W. Art and life in America. Rev. & enl. ed. N.Y., Holt, Rinehart & Winston, 1960. p. 481, col. pl. 26.

59 MARCHIORI, GIUSEPPE. La pittura straniera nelle collezioni italiane. Turin, Pozzo, 1960. n. p.
　　2 pages of text. 2 col. plates.

60 MENDELOWITZ, DANIEL M. A history of American art. N.Y., Holt, Rinehart and Winston, 1960. p. 598 incl. ill.

61 Modern artists in America. Ed. by Robert Motherwell, Ad Reinhardt. N.Y., Wittenborn Schultz [1951]. p. 27 ff*, 145 (statement), ill. p. 55.
　　* Reprint from San Francisco panel. See bibl. 67.

62 PONENTE, NELLO. Modern painting. Contemporary trends. Lausanne, Skira, 1960. p. 136–138 plus pl.

63 POUSETTE-DART, NATHANIEL, ed. American painting today. N.Y., Hastings House, 1956. p. 52, ill. p. 45.

64 RESTANY, PIERRE. Lyrisme et abstraction. Milan, Apollinaire, 1960. p. 68–70.

65 RICHARDSON, EDGAR PRESTON. Painting in America. N.Y., Thomas Y. Crowell, 1956. p. 397, ill. p. 344.

66 RODMAN, SELDEN. Conversations with artists. N.Y., Devin-Adair, 1957. p. 2–8.

67 SAN FRANCISCO ART ASSOCIATION. The western round table on modern art. Abstract of proceedings. Ed. by Douglas MacAgy. San Francisco, Art Association, 1949. 70 p.
Mimeographed. – Tobey one of the panelists.

68 SEITZ, WILLIAM C. Abstract-expressionist painting in America. 495 p. Typescript.
Diss. – Princeton, 1955.

69 SEUPHOR, MICHEL. Dictionnaire de la peinture abstraite. Paris, Hazan, 1957. p. 273–274 incl. ill.
Also English edition: Dictionary of abstract painting. N.Y., Paris Book Center, 1957. p. 273–274.

70 TAPIÉ, MICHEL. Un art autre. Paris, Gabriel-Giraud, 1952. n. p. passim.

ARTICLES ON TOBEY

71 ADLOW, DOROTHY. New York. [Mark Tobey.] *Christian Science Monitor* Nov. 23, 1957.

72 ALVARD, JULIEN. Tobey. *Cimaise* s. 2 no. 6: 3–5 ill. May 1955.

73 ASHTON, DORE. Mark Tobey. [1958.] [18] p.
Typescript.

74 ASHTON, DORE. Mark Tobey. *Evergreen Review* v. 4 no. 11: 29–36 incl. 4 col. ill. Jan.–Feb. 1960.

75 ASHTON, DORE. Mark Tobey et la rondeur parfaite. *XXe Siècle* n. s. 21 no. 12: 66–69 ill. col. pl. May–June 1959.
English summary p. [103–104].

76 BOUDAILLE, G. Tobey, peintre du Pacifique. *Les Lettres françaises* Oct. 19, 1959.

77 BOWNESS, ALAN. A synthesis in art of East and West. *The Observer* Feb. 4, 1962.

78 BRAZIER, DOROTHY BRANT. Early years of Tobey recalled. *Seattle Times* Sep. 15, 1959.

79 BREUNING, MARGARET. World's imprints on Seattle's Mark Tobey. *Art Digest* v. 26 no. 2: 11, 33 ill. Oct. 15, 1951.

80 BROOKNER, ANITA. Current and forthcoming exhibitions: London. *Burlington Magazine* v. 104 no. 708: 129 March 1962.

81 B[URREY], S[UZANNE]. Mark Tobey. *Arts* v. 32 no. 3: 53 Dec. 1957.

82 BURROWS, CARLYLE. Tobey mural faces ban by Wash. State Library. *New York Herald Tribune* March 13, 1959.

83 BURROWS, CARLYLE. Tobey's subtle talent theme of museum display. *New York Herald Tribune* Oct. 7, 1951, Section 4, p. 9.

84 CALLAHAN, MARGARET BUNDY. Mark Tobey, breaker of art traditions. *Seattle Times* Mar. 17, 1946.

85 CHEVALIER, DENYS. Une journée avec Mark Tobey. *Aujourd'hui* 6 no. 33: 4–13 ill. Oct. 1961.
See also bibl. 28.

86 CHIPP, H. B. Tobey retrospective. *Art News* 59: 58 Summer 1960.

87 CHOAY, FRANÇOISE. Un grand peintre américain expose à Paris: Mark Tobey. *France observateur* no. 402 Jan. 23, 1958.

88 COATES, R. Mazes and planes. *New Yorker* Oct. 13, 1951.

89 CORMACK, ROBIN. Mark Tobey 1925-1961. Whitechapel Art Gallery. *Arts Review* Feb. 10, 1962.

90 COURTOIS, MICHEL. Mark Tobey – des pictogrammes indiens à l'écriture blanche. *Cahiers du Musée de Poche* no. 1: 58–68 incl. ill. Mar. 1959.

91 CRISPOLTI, ENRICO. Contributi alla conoscenza dell'opera de Mark Tobey. *I 4 soli* anno 4 no. 2: 6–11 ill. Mar.–Apr. 1957.

92 DEVREE, HOWARD. An artist's growth. Mark Tobey retrospective at Whitney. *New York Times* Oct. 7, 1951 p. X 9.

93 DEVREE, HOWARD. Award at Venice. Top prize caps distinguished career of Mark Tobey. *New York Times* June 22, 1958.

94 DEVREE, HOWARD. ... Jackson Pollock and Mark Tobey. *New York Times* Dec. 3, 1950. ill.

95 DEVREE, HOWARD. Tobey art show at the Whitney. *New York Times* Oct. 4, 1951.

96 DRAPER, MURIEL. Mark Tobey. *Creative Art* v. 7 no. 4: suppl. 42–44 ill. Oct. 1930.

97 FAVRE, LOUIS-PAUL. Tobey. *Réforme* Jan. 16, 1960.

98 F[ITZSIMMONS], J[AMES]. Mark Tobey. *Art Digest* v. 27 no. 14: 16 Apr. 15 ,1953.

99 FLANNER, JANET. Tobey, mystique errant. *L'Oeil* no. 6: 26–31 ill. June 15, 1955.
Translated into English: "Sage from Wisconsin." *Selective Eye* 1955: 170–175 ill.

100 FRANKENSTEIN, ALFRED. Tobey and Bertoia: Fantasy and geometry. *Art News* v. 44 no. 12: 28 ill. Oct. 1–14, 1945.

101 FRIED, ALEXANDER. Early work key to Tobey art. *San Francisco Examiner* Apr. 22, 1951.

102 FRIED, MICHAEL. White writing and pop art. *Arts Magazine* v. 36 no. 7: 26–28 incl. ill. Apr. 1962.

103 GAUNT, WILLIAM. The painter as calligrapher. *Sunday Telegraph* Feb. 4, 1962.

104 GENAUER, EMILY. [Mark Tobey.] *New York World Telegram* Apr. 8, 1944.

105 GIBBS, JO. Tobey the Mystic. *Art Digest* v. 20 no. 4:39 Nov. 15, 1945.

106 GRAHAM, HUGH. Mark Tobey. *The Spectator,* Feb. 9, 1962.

107 GREENBERG, CLEMENT. "Art." *Nation* 158:495 Apr. 22, 1944.

108 HAGAN, YVONNE. Mark Tobey. *New York Herald Tribune* (Paris) Dec. 22, 1954.

109 Hällristningar lockar målare från Amerika. (Rockcarvings attract painter from America) *Göteborgs-Posten* Aug. 26, 1954.
    In Swedish.

110 JEANNERAT, PIERRE. Human ants in a waste of nothing. *The Daily Mail* Feb. 2, 1962.

111 JOUFFROY, ALAIN. Marc Tobey. *Arts* (Paris) no. 509:11 Mar. 30–Apr. 5, 1955.

112 KOCHNITZKY, LÉON. Mark Tobey. *Quadrum* no. 4:14–26 ill. col. pl. 1957.
    English summary p. 192–193.

113 K[RASNE] B[ELLE]. A Tobey profile. *Art Digest* v. 26 no. 2:5, 26, 34 Oct. 15, 1951.

114 LACOSTE, MICHEL CONIL. Tobey. *Le Monde* Mar. 25, 1955.

115 LACOSTE, MICHEL CONIL. Rétrospective Mark Tobey. *Le Monde* Oct. 24, 1961.

116 LUCIE-SMITH, EDWARD. White magic. *New Statesman* Feb. 16, 1962.

117 LUNDKVIST, ARTHUR. Mark Tobey from Seattle. *Stockholms-Tidningen* Apr. 28, 1960.

118 MC BRIDE, HENRY. Abstract report for April. *Art News* v. 52 no. 2:16–18, 47 Apr. 1953.

119 Mark Tobey's Red Man–White Man–Black Man. *Buffalo Fine Arts Academy Gallery Notes* v. 11 no. 3:25–29 ill. June 1947.

120 MELVILLE, ROBERT. Exhibitions. *Architectural Review* v. 131 no. 782:281–282 incl. ill. April 1962.

121 Memories of Emily Carr in a Tobey exhibition. *Canadian Art* 16:274 Nov. 1959.

122 MULLALY, TERENCE. Mark Tobey's art offers solace to the baffled. *The Daily Telegraph* Feb. 2, 1962.

123 NEWTON, ERIC. At Whitechapel. *The Guardian* Feb. 1, 1962.

124 Northwest passage. *Newsweek* Sept. 10, 1945. ill. port.

125 OERI, GEORGINE. Tobey and Rothko. *Baltimore Museum of Art News* v. 23 no. 2:2–6 ill. Winter 1960.

126 Old master of America's new painting. *The Stars and Stripes* (Germany) Jan. 11, 1961, p. 11, ill. port.

127 PRIOR, HARRIS K. The Pacific Northwest. *The League Quarterly* v. 21 no. 2:18–23 ill. Winter 1949.

128 The private art of Mark Tobey. *The Times* (London) Feb. 1, 1962.

129 PUTMAN, JACQUES. Mark Tobey et l'École du Pacifique. *France observateur* Oct. 26, 1961.

130 RAGON, MICHEL. A 70 ans Tobey est révélé par Paris. *Arts* (Paris) no. 839:6 Oct. 18–24, 1961.

131 REED, JUDITH KAYE. Tobey's variations. *Art Digest* v. 24 no. 4:16 Nov. 15, 1949.

132 RESTANY, PIERRE. Tobey. *Cimaise* s. 5 no. 4:41 Mar.–Apr. 1958.

133 REXROTH, KENNETH. Mark Tobey of Seattle, Wash. *Art News* v. 50 no. 3:16–19, 61 ill. May 1951.

134 R[ILEY], M[AUDE]. Tobey's white writing. *Art Digest* v. 18 no. 13:19 Apr. 1, 1944.

135 ROBERTS, COLETTE. Affirmations: Tobey et Soulages. *France-Amérique* Nov. 24, 1957.

136 ROBERTS, KEITH. The time and the space. *Time & Tide* Feb. 8, 1962.

137 SCHNEIDER, PIERRE. Paris: Limits of style: Luce, Tobey. *Art News* v. 57 no. 1:46, 54 Mar. 1958.

138 SCHULZ, PHOEBE. Mark Tobey. *Das Kunstwerk* Jahrg. 11 no. 3:24–30, 35–36 ill. Sept. 1957.

139 A Seattle painter wins top European prize. *Life* v. 45 no. 3:50–51 ill. July 21, 1958.

140 Seattle tangler. *Time* Apr. 9, 1951, p. 86 incl. ill.

141 Tobey, Mark. *Current biography* v. 18 no. 3:58–60 Mar. 1957.
    Also: Current biography yearbook 1957, p. 553–555.

142 Tobey exhibition, Marian Willard's Gallery. *Art News* 44:24 Dec. 1, 1945.

143 Tobey retrospective at the Pasadena Museum. *Art News* 59:51 Mar. 1960.

144 TOOMEY, TOM. Mark Tobey. *The Town Crier* (Seattle) Aug. 1, 1931, p. 7, 9.

145 "Two Men" and "Flow of the night" acquired by the museum. *Portland Art Museum Bulletin* v. 7 no. 3:2 Nov. 1945.

146 T[YLER], P[ARKER]. Mark Tobey. *Art News* v. 53 no. 7:51 Nov. 1954.

147 WATT, ALEXANDER. Paris commentary. *The Studio* v. 162 no. 824:222–224, 235 ill. Dec. 1961.
    Statements by Tobey in the text.

148 WATT, ALEXANDER. Paris letter: Mark Tobey. *Art in America* no. 4:112–114 ill. 1961.

149 WEELEN, GUY. Un Oriental en Occident: Mark Tobey. *Les Lettres françaises* n.d. 1961.

150 WIEGAND, CHARMION VON. The vision of Mark Tobey. *Arts* (New York) v. 33 no. 10:34–41 ill. Sept. 1959.

151 ZERVOS, CHRISTIAN. Mark Tobey. *Cahiers d'Art* 29 no. 2:260–263 ill. 1954.

ARTICLES, GENERAL

(Pages marked * refer specifically to Tobey)

152 ALVARD, JULIEN. Potentiel américain. *Cimaise* s. 4 no. 2:29–31, Nov.–Dec. 1956.

153 ASHTON, DORE. New Japanese "Abstract calligraphy." *Art Digest* v. 28 no. 19:24–25 Aug. 1, 1954.

154 CALLAHAN, KENNETH. Pacific Northwest. *Art News* v. 45 no. 5:22–27, 53–55 ill. July 1946.

155 CHOAY, FRANÇOISE. La XXIXe Biennale de Venise. *L'Oeil* no. 45:28–35 Sept. 1958.

156 COURTOIS, MICHEL. De la calligraphie orientale à l'art abstrait. *Arts* (Paris) no. 562:12 Apr. 4–10, 1956.

157 "L'ÉCOLE DU PACIFIQUE." [Symposium.] *Cimaise* no. 7:6–9 ill. June 1954.

158 GOLDWATER, ROBERT. Reflections on the New York school. *Quadrum* 8:17–36, 1960.

159 GREENBERG, CLEMENT. "American type" painting. *Partisan Review* v. 22 no. 2:179–196 (*187–188) Spring 1955.

160 GREENBERG, CLEMENT. The present prospects of American painting and sculpture. *Horizon* v. 16 no. 93/94:20–30 (*25) Oct. 1947.

161 GREENE, BALCOMB. Fourteen Americans. *MKR's art outlook* Oct. 7, 1946.

162 HAYES, BARTLETT H., JR. The root of American painting. *Art News* v. 56 no. 9:28–31, 61–62 (*31, 61) ill. Jan. 1958.

163 HERON, PATRICK. London. *Arts* v. 32 no. 4:18 Jan. 1958.

164 JOHNSON, UNA E. Contemporary American drawings. *Perspectives U. S. A.* no. 13:89–99 (*99) ill. Fall 1955.

165 KOCHNITZKY, LÉON. De quelques peintres américains de ce temps. *Les Beaux-Arts* (Brussels) no. 686:3,5 Apr. 1, 1955.

166 LEGRAND, FRANCINE-CLAIRE. La peinture et la sculpture au défi. *Quadrum* 7:23–52 (*33–34) ill. 1959.
English summary p. 186–189.

167 Mark Tobey. *Art News* v. 43 no. 5:25 Apr. 15–30, 1944.

168 MATHIEU, GEORGES. Towards a new convergence of art, thought and science. *Art International* v. 4 no. 4:26–47 May 1, 1960.

169 MELQUIST, JEROME. Un nouveau point de rencontre entre l'Occident et l'Orient. *Prisme des Arts* no. 6:30–32 Nov. 1956.

170 MUNSTERBERG, HUGO. East and West in contemporary Japanese art. *College Art Journal* 18 no. 1:36–41 Fall 1958.

171 Mystic painters of the Northwest. *Life* v. 35 no. 13:84–89 ill. Sept. 28, 1953.

172 Northwest painting (Austin, Tobey, van Cott, M. Graves). *Fortune* v. 31 no. 2:164–168 ill. Feb. 1945.

173 RAGON, MICHEL. Art today in the United States. *Cimaise* s. 6 no. 3:6–35 incl. ill. Jan.–Mar. 1959.

174 RENZIO, TONI DEL. The grass code of art. *Art News and Review* v. 7 no. 8:8 May 14, 1955.

175 RESTANY, PIERRE. L'Amérique aux Américains. *Ring des Arts* 1960:23–31 (*26–27) ill.

176 SAWYER, KENNETH. L'expressionisme abstrait. La phase du Pacifique. *Cimaise* no. 7:3–5 June 1954.

177 SEELEY, CAROL. On the nature of abstract painting in America. *Magazine of Art* v. 43 no. 5:163–168 (*166, 168) ill. May 1950.

178 SEITZ, WILLIAM. Spirit, time and "abstract expressionism." *Magazine of Art* v. 46 no. 2:80–88 (*84–86) Feb. 1953.

179 SEUPHOR, MICHEL. Paris–New York 1951. *Art d'aujourd'hui* s. 2 no. 6:4–15 ill. June 1951.
Entire issue devoted to "La peinture aux Etats-Unis."

180 STRATER, HENRY. Pacific northwest painters and sculptors. *In* Museum of Art of Ogunquit, Fifth annual exhibition, June 29–Sept. 9, 1957. p. [5–7].
Commentary to "Meditative Series # 7."

181 SUNLEY, ROBERT. Fourteen American artists. *Critique* v. 1 no. 1:18–21 Oct. 1946.

182 TAPIÉ, MICHEL. Messages sans étiquette. *XXe Siècle* n. s. no. 5:17–24 ill. June 1955.

183 WANKMÜLLER, RIKE. Tachisten in U. S. A. *Kunstwerk* v. 9 no. 5:23–26 1955/56.

184 WRIGHT, CLIFFORD. The American dream world: a mystery of space. *Studio* 157:16–19 Jan. 1959.

BAHÁ'Í & ZEN

185 Bahá'í world faith. Selected writings by Bahá'u'lláh and 'Abdu'l-Bahá. 2d ed. Wilmette, Ill., Bahá'í Publishing Trust, c. 1956.

186 DORFLES, GILLO. Lo Zen e l'arte d'oggi. *Domus* no. 366:25–26 May 1960.

187 KUNZ, ANNA. A Bahá'í in Switzerland. Excerpts from letters to her daughters. *World Order* v. 14 no. 12:399–411 March 1949.

188 MUNSTERBERG, HUGO. Zen and art. *Art Journal* 20 no. 4:198–202 Summer 1961.

189 ROSS, NANCY WILSON. The square roots of Zen. *Horizon* v. 1 no. 6:70–77, 126 incl. ill. July 1959.

190 ROSS, NANCY WILSON. What is Zen? *Mademoiselle* Jan. 1958.
Discusses Tobey and Graves.

191 ROSS, NANCY WILSON. The world of Zen. N. Y., Random House, 1960.

192 SUZUKI, DAISETZ TEITARO. Sengai: Zen and art. *Art News Annual* 27:116–121 ff. Winter 1958/59.

SELECTED CATALOGUES *(arranged chronologically)*

193 WILLARD GALLERY, NEW YORK. Mark Tobey. N.Y., 1944.
[4]p.
> Exhibition Apr. 4–29, 1944. – 19 works. – Includes text
> on Tobey by Sidney Janis.

194 PORTLAND ART MUSEUM. Paintings by Mark Tobey. Portland, Oregon. 1945. [15]p. incl. ill.
> Exhibition July 7–Aug. 12, 1945. – 31 works. Circulated
> to San Francisco Art Museum, Arts Club of Chicago,
> Detroit Institute of Arts. – Statement by the artist p.
> [3–5]. – Comments by Julia und Lyonel Feininger.

195 NEW YORK. MUSEUM OF MODERN ART. Fourteen Americans.
Ed. by Dorothy C. Miller. N.Y., 1946. 80p. incl. ill.
> Exhibition Sept. 10–Dec. 8, 1946. – 14 works by Tobey. –
> Tobey p. 70–75 incl. ill. – Statement by Tobey p. 70.

196 WILLARD GALLERY, NEW YORK. Tobey. N.Y., 1947. [5]p.
incl. ill.
> Exhibition Nov. 4–29, 1947. – 21 works.

197 WILLARD GALLERY, NEW YORK. Mark Tobey. N.Y., 1949.
[8]p. incl. ill.
> Exhibition Nov. 1–26, 1949. – 17 works. – Note by the
> artist p. [3].

198 SAN FRANCISCO. CALIFORNIA PALACE OF THE LEGION OF
HONOR. Retrospective exhibition of paintings by Mark Tobey. San Francisco, 1951. [24]p. incl. ill.
> Exhibition Mar. 31–May 6, 1951. – 96 works. – Introduc-
> tion by Jermayne MacAgy p. [2–3]. – Some statements
> by the artist p. [4].

199 NEW YORK. WHITNEY MUSEUM OF AMERICAN ART. Mark
Tobey. Retrospective exhibition. N.Y., 1951. [24]p. incl.
ill. port.
> Exhibition Oct. 4–Nov. 4, 1951. – 70 works. – Foreword
> by Hermon More p. [3]. – "Tobey's story" (including
> statements by the artist) p. [4–7] by Jermayne MacAgy.

200 WILLARD GALLERY, NEW YORK. Tobey. N.Y., 1953. [5]p.
incl. ill.
> Exhibition Apr. 1–May 2, 1953. – 12 works.

201 LONDON. INSTIUTE OF CONTEMPORARY ARTS. Mark Tobey.
London, 1955. [9] p. ill.
> Exhibition May 4–June 4, 1955. – 33 works. – Introduc-
> tion by Lawrence Alloway.

202 HOUSTON. CONTEMPORARY ARTS MUSEUM. Contemporary
calligraphers: John Marin, Mark Tobey, Morris Graves.
Houston, 1956. [30] p. incl. ill.
> Exhibition Apr. 12–May 13, 1956. – 17 works by Tobey.
> – Foreword by Frederick S. Wight. – Includes statements
> by Tobey.

203 NEW YORK. MUSEUM OF MODERN ART. INTERNATIONAL
COUNCIL. Lipton, Rothko, Smith, Tobey. XXIX Biennale,
Venezia 1958: Stati Uniti d'America. N.Y., 1958. [53] p.
incl. ill.
> Exhibition June 14–Oct. 19, 1958. – 36 works by Tobey.
> – Preface by Porter A. McCray. – "Mark Tobey" by
> Frank O'Hara.

204 NEW YORK. WHITNEY MUSEUM OF AMERICAN ART. The Museum and its friends. Eighteen living American artists . . .
N.Y., 1959. 50p. incl. ill.
> Exhibition Mar. 5–Apr. 12, 1959. – 4 works by Tobey. –
> Includes Tobey statement from "Reminiscence and Rev-
> erie" p. 39. See bibl. 9.

205 ST. ALBANS SCHOOL, WASHINGTON, D.C. Fiftieth anniversary celebration exhibition May 21–June 3, 1959. p. 7–12
(The Tobey section by Arthur Hall Smith).

206 SEATTLE. ART MUSEUM. Mark Tobey: a retrospective exhibition from Northwest collections. Seattle, 1959. [22] p.
incl. ill.
> Exhibition Sept. 11–Nov. 1, 1959. – 224 works. – Text by
> Edward B. Thomas. – Circulated to Portland, Colorado
> Springs, Pasadena, San Francisco.

207 MANNHEIM. KUNSTHALLE. Mark Tobey. Mannheim, 1960.
[12] p. plus ill. (some col.).
> Exhibition Dec. 17, 1960–Jan. 22, 1961. – 121 works. –
> Includes excerpt in translation of a letter from Tobey,
> part of which is also given in facsimile.

208 BEYELER, GALERIE, BASEL. Mark Tobey. Basel, 1961 [12]p.
plus 31 ill. (pt. col.).
> Exhibition May–June 1961. – 52 works. – Comments by
> a fellow artist by Julia and Lyonel Feininger p. [2–3]
> (also in German). – Biography and bibliography (in Ger-
> man). – Contains statements by Tobey throughout (some
> in English, some in French, some in German).

209 PARIS. MUSÉE DES ARTS DÉCORATIFS. Mark Tobey. Paris,
1961. [108] p. plus 91 ill. (some col.).
> Exhibition Oct. 18–Dec. 1, 1961. – 286 works. – Includes
> "textes de Tobey," bibliography and list of exhibitions. –
> Also shown at The Whitechapel Gallery, London, 1962. –
> 183 works. – Catalogue an abbreviated translation of the
> French original.

FILM

210 Mark Tobey: Artist. Seattle, Orbit Films, 1952.
> Directed by Robert G. Gardner, music and script by
> Mark Tobey; photographer William Hieck. 16 mm; color;
> sound; 20 min. Available from Brandon Films, 200 W.
> 57 St., N.Y.

Mr. and Mrs. Hans Arnhold, New York; Hollis S. Baker, Grand Rapids, Michigan; Mr. and Mrs. Arthur G. Barnett, Seattle; Mr. and Mrs. Arthur L. Dahl, Pebble Beach, California; Mr. and Mrs. Harold Diamond, New York; Mrs. Lyonel Feininger, New York; Mr. and Mrs. Paul Feldenheimer, Portland, Oregon; Carol Ely Harper, Seattle; Mr. and Mrs. John H. Hauberg, Jr., Seattle; Mr. and Mrs. Ira Haupt, Asbury Park, New Jersey; Mrs. Kay Hillman, New York; The Joseph H. Hirshhorn Foundation Inc., New York; Colonel and Mrs. A. H. Hooker, Jr., Tacoma, Washington; Rudolph Indlekofer, Basel; O'Donnell Iselin, New York; Mrs. Martha Jackson, New York; Berthe Poncy Jacobson, Seattle; Dan R. Johnson, New York; Marian Willard Johnson, New York; Mr. and Mrs. C. Ron Johnsone, Seattle; Carolyn Kizer, Seattle; Benjamin H. Kizer, Spokane, Washington; Mr. and Mrs. Sigmund Kunstadter, Highland Park, Illinois; Mr. and Mrs. Richard Lippold, Locust Valley, New York; Wright Ludington, Santa Barbara, California; Mr. and Mrs. Arnold H. Maremont, Chicago; Mrs. Joyce Markson, New York; Mr. and Mrs. Ambrose McCarthy, Patterson, Seattle; N. Richard Miller, New York; Mr. and Mrs. Roy R. Neuberger, New York; Mrs. Albert H. Newman, Chicago; Mr. and Mrs. Andrew E. Norman, Palisades, New York; Robert Norton, New York; Governor Nelson A. Rockefeller, New York; Mr. and Mrs. Sam Rubinstein, Seattle; Albert Ruddock, Santa Barbara; Mr. and Mrs. Daniel Saidenberg, New York; Nathaniel Saltonstall, Boston; Otto D. Seligman, Seattle; Mr. and Mrs. Joseph R. Shapiro, Oak Park, Illinois; Herman Shulman Collection, New York; Mr. and Mrs. Solomon B. Smith, Lake Forest, Illinois; Mr. and Mrs. Olin J. Stephens II, Scarsdale, New York; Mrs. Thomas D. Stimson, Seattle; G. David Thompson, Pittsburgh; Mark Tobey, Seattle; Mr. and Mrs. Burton Tremaine, Meriden, Connecticut; Mr. and Mrs. Windsor Utley, Seattle; Mr. and Mrs. James W. Washington, Jr., Seattle; Dr. and Mrs. Benjamin Philp Watson, Danbury, Connecticut; Mr. and Mrs. Max Weinstein, Seattle; Mr. and Mrs. Harry Lewis Winston, Birmingham, Michigan.

Addison Gallery of American Art, Phillips Academy, Andover, Massachusetts; The Baltimore Museum of Art; Museum of Fine Arts, Boston; Albright-Knox Art Gallery, Buffalo; The Art Institute of Chicago; The Detroit Institute of Arts; Wadsworth Atheneum, Hartford; Milwaukee Art Center; The Brooklyn Museum, New York; The Metropolitan Museum of Art, New York; The Museum of Modern Art, New York; Whitney Museum of American Art, New York; Carnegie Institute, Pittsburgh; Portland Art Museum, Portland, Oregon; San Francisco Museum of Art; City Art Museum of St. Louis; Seattle Art Museum; Munson-Williams-Proctor Institute, Utica; The Phillips Collection, Washington; Norton Gallery and School of Art, West Palm Beach, Florida.

Galerie Beyeler, Basel; Galerie Jeanne Bucher, Paris; Zoe Dusanne Gallery, Seattle; Sidney Janis Gallery, New York; Royal Marks Gallery, New York; Galerie Saqqârah, Gstaad, Switzerland; Otto Seligman Gallery, Seattle; Willard Gallery, New York.

EXHIBITION DATES

The Museum of Modern Art, New York: *September 12 – November 4, 1962*

The Cleveland Museum of Art: *December 11, 1962 – January 13, 1963*

The Art Institute of Chicago: *February 22 – March 24, 1963*

Dates enclosed in parentheses do not appear on the paintings. In dimensions height precedes width. Works marked with an asterisk are illustrated.

* 1 *Conflict of the Satanic and Celestial Egos.* (c. 1918). Watercolor on cardboard, 18¹/₂ × 12″. Owned by the artist. Ill. p. 10

2 *Portrait of Paul McCool.* 1925. Conte crayon on paper, 24 × 18¹/₄″. Signed and dated lower right. Collection Mrs. Thomas D. Stimson, Seattle

3 *Rainy Day.* (c. 1925). Pencil on paper, 18 × 21¹/₂″. Collection Robert Norton, New York

* 4 *Cirque d'Hiver.* (1933). Pastel, 16⁷/₈ × 21¹/₂″. Collection Mr. and Mrs. Windsor Utley, Seattle. Ill. p. 21

5 *Adam and Eve.* (c. 1934). Tempera on paper, 8¹/₄ × 3³/₄″. Collection Carolyn Kizer, Seattle

* 6 *Three Birds.* 1934 (?). Tempera on paper, 10³/₄ × 14⁷/₈″. Signed and dated lower right "Tobey/35." Seattle Art Museum. Eugene Fuller Memorial Collection. Ill. p. 50

* 7 *Broadway.* (1935?). Tempera on composition board, 26 × 19¹/₄″. Signed lower right "Tobey/36" (see note 47). The Metropolitan Museum of Art. Arthur H. Hearn Fund, 1942. (Exhibited in New York only). Ill. p. 17

* 8 *Broadway Norm.* 1935 (?). Tempera on cardboard, 13¹/₄ × 9³/₈″. Signed and dated lower left and lower right (see note 47). Collection Carol Ely Harper, Seattle. Ill. p. 51.

9 *Interior of the Studio.* (1937). Tempera, 17¹/₂ × 22¹/₂″. Collection Mr. and Mrs. Ambrose McCarthy, Patterson, Seattle

*10 *Five sketches, Pike Place Public Market, Seattle.* 1941. Watercolor and ink on paper, 8⁵/₈ × 5⁵/₈″ each. Seattle Art Museum. Eugene Fuller Memorial Collection. Ill. p. 93

11 *Two Men.* 1941. Tempera on paper, 11⁵/₈ × 9″. Signed and dated lower right. Portland Art Museum, Portland, Oregon

*12 *Forms Follow Man.* (1941). Tempera on cardboard, 13⁵/₈ × 19⁵/₈″. Signed and dated lower right "Tobey/43" (see note 47). Seattle Art Museum. Eugene Fuller Memorial Collection. Ill. p. 54

13 *San Francisco Street.* (1941). Tempera, 27¹/₄ × 13″. Detroit Institute of Arts

*14 *The Void Devouring the Gadget Era.* 1942. Tempera on paper, 21¹/₂ × 29³/₈″. Signed and dated lower right. Owned by the artist. Ill. p. 11

*15 *Remembrance in Light.* (1942). Tempera on paper, 13³/₈ × 9³/₈″. Signed lower right. Collection Col. and Mrs. A. H. Hooker, Jr., Tacoma, Washington. Ill. p. 36

*16 *Threading Light.* 1942. Tempera on cardboard, 29³/₈ × 19¹/₂″. Signed and dated lower right. The Museum of Modern Art, New York. Ill. p. 55

17 *In the Marsh.* 1942. Tempera on paper, 15 × 9¹/₂″. Signed and dated lower right. Collection O'Donnell Iselin, New York

*18 *Drift of Summer.* 1942. Tempera, 28 × 22″. Signed and dated lower right. Collection Wright Ludington, Santa Barbara, California. (Exhibited in New York only). Ill. p. 57

*19 *Broadway Boogie.* 1942. Tempera on composition board, 31³/₈ × 24³/₈″. Signed and dated upper right. Collection Mr. and Mrs. Max Weinstein, Seattle. Ill. p. 26

*20 *E Pluribus Unum.* 1942 (or 1943). Tempera on paper, 20¹/₈ × 24¹/₂″. Signed upper right "Tobey/42." Seattle Art Museum. Gift of Mrs. Thomas D. Stimson. Ill. p. 32

*21 *Flow of the Night.* 1943. Tempera on cardboard, 20³/₄ × 15¹/₂″. Signed and dated lower right. Portland Art Museum, Portland, Oregon. Ill. p. 61

22 *Sale.* 1943. Tempera on composition board, 18 × 29⁷/₈″. Signed and dated lower left. Whitney Museum of American Art, New York. Gift of Mr. and Mrs. David M. Solinger

23 *Cubist Vertical.* 1943. Tempera, 17 × 6″. Signed and dated lower right. Collection Albert Ruddock, Santa Barbara, California

*24 *Gothic.* 1943. Tempera on paper, 27³/₄ × 21⁵/₈″. Signed and dated upper left. Collection Berthe Poncy Jacobson, Seattle. Ill. p. 58

*25 *Pacific Transition.* 1943. Tempera on composition board, 23¹/₄ × 31¹/₄″. Signed and dated lower right. City Art Museum of St. Louis. Ill. p. 59

26 *Christmas Night.* 1943. Tempera on paper, 15 × 20¹/₄″. Signed and dated lower right. Collection Berthe Poncy Jacobson, Seattle

*27 *Western Town.* 1944. Tempera on paper, 12 × 18³/₄″. Signed and dated lower right. Collection Mr. and Mrs. Paul Feldenheimer, Portland, Oregon. Ill. p. 63

28 *World Egg.* 1944. Tempera, 19 × 24″. Signed and dated lower right. Collection Carolyn Kizer, Seattle

*29 *Remote Field.* 1944. Tempera, pencil and crayon on cardboard, 28¹/₈ × 30¹/₈″. Signed and dated lower right. The Museum of Modern Art, New York. Gift of Mr. and Mrs. Jan de Graaff. Ill. p. 63

*30 *The Way.* 1944. Tempera on paper, 13⁷/₈ × 22¹/₈″. Signed and dated lower right. Collection Mrs. Albert H. Newman, Chicago. Ill. p. 62

*31 *Voice of the Doll.* 1944. Tempera on paper, 19¹/₂ × 7¹/₂″. Signed and dated lower right. Collection Marian Willard Johnson, New York. Ill. p. 34

*32 *City Radiance*. 1944. Tempera on paper, 19³/₈×14¹/₄″. Signed and dated lower right. Collection Mrs. Lyonel Feininger, New York. Ill. p. 64

*33 *New York*. 1944. Tempera on cardboard, 33×21″. Signed and dated lower right. Collection Marian Willard Johnson, New York. Ill. p. 65

34 *Crystallization*. (1944). Tempera on paper, 18×13″. Collection Dr. and Mrs. Benjamin Philp Watson, Danbury, Connecticut

35 *Electric Night*. 1944. Tempera on paper, 17³/₄×13⁵/₈″. Signed and dated lower right. Seattle Art Museum. Eugene Fuller Memorial Collection

36 *Pattern of Conflict*. 1944. Tempera on paper, 13⁵/₈×19¹/₂″. Signed and dated lower right. Collection Mr. and Mrs. Burton Tremaine, Meriden, Connecticut

37 *Tundra*. 1944. Tempera on paper, 24×16¹/₂″. Signed and dated lower right. Collection Mr. and Mrs. Roy R. Neuberger, New York

*38 *Drums, Indians and the Word of God*. 1944. Tempera on wood, 18¹/₂×13⁷/₈″. Signed and dated lower right. Herman Shulman Collection, New York. Ill. p. 66

39 *Totemic Disturbance*. 1945. Tempera on paper, 14×24¹/₂″. Signed and dated lower right. Collection Carolyn Kizer, Seattle

40 *Red Man – White Man – Black Man*. 1945. Oil and tempera on cardboard, 25×28″. Signed and dated lower right. Room of Contemporary Art Collection, Albright-Knox Art Gallery, Buffalo

*41 *The New Day*. 1945(?). Tempera on paper, 12³/₄×23¹/₄″. Signed and dated lower right "Tobey/40." Collection Mr. and Mrs. Arthur L. Dahl, Pebble Beach, California. Ill. p. 12

*42 *Lines of the City*. 1945. Tempera on paper, 17¹/₂×21³/₄″. Signed and dated lower right. Addison Gallery of American Art, Phillips Academy, Andover, Massachusetts. Ill. p. 64

43 *November Grass Rhythms*. 1945. Tempera on cardboard, 19¹/₄×15″. Signed and dated lower right. Collection Carol Ely Harper, Seattle

44 *Agate World*. 1945. Tempera on cardboard, 14⁷/₈×11″. Signed and dated lower right. Seattle Art Museum. Gift of Eunice P. Clise Fund, Seattle Foundation

45 *Eskimo Idiom*. 1946. Tempera on paper, 43¹/₂×27³/₄″. Signed and dated lower right. Collection Mr. and Mrs. Sam Rubinstein, Seattle

46 *Silent Flight*. 1946. Tempera on wood, 24¹/₂×18″. Signed and dated lower right. Sidney Janis Gallery, New York

*47 *New York Tablet*. 1946. Tempera on paper, 24⁷/₈×19″. Signed and dated lower right. Munson-Williams-Proctor Institute, Utica. Edward W. Root Bequest. Ill. p. 25

48 *Prophetic Plane*. 1947. Tempera on paper, 25¹/₄×19¹/₈″. Signed and dated lower right. Collection Hollis S. Baker, Grand Rapids, Michigan

49 *Island Memories*. 1947. Tempera on paper, 24×18¹/₄″. Signed and dated lower right. The Brooklyn Museum, New York

*50 *Arena of Civilization*. 1947. Tempera on cardboard, 14×19³/₄″. Signed and dated lower left. Collection Mrs. Martha Jackson, New York. Ill. p. 37

*51 *The Retreat of the Friend*. (1947). Tempera, 10×14³/₄″. Signed lower right. Collection Nathaniel Saltonstall, Boston. Ill. p. 13

*52 *Homage to the Virgin*. 1948. Tempera on paper, 9×15″. Signed and dated lower right. Collection Mr. and Mrs. Daniel Saidenberg, New York. Ill. p. 69

53 *Echoes from the Orient*. 1948. Tempera, 6¹/₈×15⁷/₈″. Signed and dated lower right. Collection Otto D. Seligman, Seattle

*54 *Tropicalism*. 1948. Oil and tempera on paper, 26¹/₂×19³/₄″. Signed and dated lower right. Galerie Saqqârah, Gstaad, Switzerland. Ill. p. 66

55 *Geography of Phantasy*. 1948. Tempera on paper, 20×26″. Signed and dated lower right. Collection Mr. and Mrs. Olin J. Stephens II, Scarsdale, New York

56 *Transit*. 1948. Tempera on cardboard, 24¹/₂×18¹/₂″. Signed and dated lower right. The Metropolitan Museum of Art. George A. Hearn Fund, 1949. (Exhibited in New York only)

57 *Self-Portrait*. 1949. Pastel, 19¹/₈×13¹/₂″. Signed and dated lower right. Zoe Dusanne Gallery, Seattle

58 *Self-Portrait*. 1949. Tempera, 17¹/₄×12¹/₈″. Signed and dated lower right. Collection Mr. and Mrs. James W. Washington, Jr., Seattle

*59 *Family*. 1949. Tempera, 12×7¹/₂″. Signed and dated lower right. Collection Marian Willard Johnson, New York. Ill. p. 68

*60 *Universal Field*. 1949. Tempera and pastel on cardboard, 28×48¹/₈″. Signed and dated lower right. Whitney Museum of American Art, New York. Ill. p. 28

61 *Awakening Night*. 1949. Tempera on composition board, 20×27¹/₈″. Signed and dated lower right. Munson-Williams-Proctor Institute, Utica. Edward W. Root Bequest

*62 *Portrait of Benjamin H. Kizer*. (1950). Tempera, 11¹/₂×7¹/₈″. Collection Carolyn Kizer, Seattle. Ill. p. 35

*63 *Written Over the Plains*. 1950. Oil and tempera on composition board, 29⁷/₈×39⁵/₈″. Signed and dated lower left. San Francisco Museum of Art. Gift of Mrs. Ferdinand Smith. Ill. p. 71

64 *Broadway Afternoon*. 1950. Watercolor, 19¹/₄×25″. Signed and dated lower right. Wadsworth Atheneum, Hartford,

Ella Gallup Sumner, Mary Catlin Sumner Collection

65 *Pacific Cloud.* 1950. Tempera on paper, $15^{1}/_{4} \times 20^{3}/_{4}''$. Signed and dated lower right. Seattle Art Museum. Eugene Fuller Memorial Collection

*66 *Aerial City.* 1950. Watercolor, $16^{1}/_{8} \times 19^{3}/_{4}''$. Signed and dated lower right. Collection Mrs. Lyonel Feininger, New York. Ill. p. 70

*67 *Canal of Cultures.* 1951. Tempera, $19^{1}/_{2} \times 25^{3}/_{4}''$. Signed and dated lower right. Collection Benjamin H. Kizer, Spokane, Washington. Ill. p. 70

*68 *Universal City.* (1951). Tempera on paper, $34^{3}/_{8} \times 24^{7}/_{8}''$. Collection Marian Willard Johnson, New York. Ill. p. 29

*69 *1951.* 1951. Tempera on paper, $43^{3}/_{4} \times 27^{3}/_{4}''$. Signed lower right "Tobey/51." Collection Mr. and Mrs. Joseph R. Shapiro, Oak Park, Illinois. Ill. p. 74

70 *The Street.* 1952. Tempera on paper, $41^{1}/_{2} \times 32^{5}/_{8}''$. Signed and dated lower right. Collection Mrs. Joyce Markson, New York

*71 *Delta.* 1952. Oil and tempera on cardboard, $43^{1}/_{2} \times 27^{5}/_{8}''$. Signed and dated lower right. Collection Dan R. Johnson, New York. Ill. p. 67

*72 *Voyage of the Saints.* 1952. Tempera and crayon on cardboard, $21 \times 27''$. Signed and dated lower right. Munson-Williams-Proctor Institute, Utica. Edward W. Root Bequest. Ill. p. 72

*73 *Omnia.* 1952. Tempera, $28^{1}/_{2} \times 29^{1}/_{2}''$. Signed and dated lower right. Collection Mr. and Mrs. Sigmund Kunstadter, Highland Park, Illinois. Ill. p. 24

*74 *Above the Earth.* 1953. Tempera on cardboard, $39^{1}/_{4} \times 29^{3}/_{4}''$. Signed and dated lower right. The Art Institute of Chicago. Gift of Mr. and Mrs. Sigmund Kunstadter. Ill. p. 75

*75 *Edge of August.* 1953. Tempera on composition board, $48 \times 28''$. Signed and dated lower right. The Museum of Modern Art, New York. Ill. p. 39

76 *Northwest Phantasy.* 1953. Tempera on paper, $41^{3}/_{4} \times 47^{1}/_{2}''$. Signed and dated lower left. Collection Mr. and Mrs. John H. Hauberg, Jr., Seattle

77 *The Window.* 1953. Tempera on cardboard, $44 \times 28''$. Signed and dated lower right. Collection Mr. and Mrs. Arnold H. Maremont, Chicago

78 *Space Line.* 1953. Tempera on paper, $26^{5}/_{8} \times 5^{7}/_{8}''$. Signed and dated lower right. Willard Gallery, New York

79 *Breath of Stone.* 1954. Tempera on paper, $12 \times 6^{1}/_{2}''$. Signed and dated lower right. Collection Mrs. Kay Hillman, New York

*80 *Meditative Series VIII.* 1954. Tempera on paper, $17^{3}/_{4} \times 11^{3}/_{4}''$. Signed and dated lower right. Collection Mr. and Mrs. Arthur L. Dahl, Pebble Beach, California. Ill. p. 76

81 *From the "Meditative Series."* (1954). Tempera on paper, $15^{1}/_{4} \times 10''$. Galerie Beyeler, Basel

82 *Unknown Field.* (1954). Tempera on paper, $11^{1}/_{4} \times 7^{1}/_{4}''$. Royal Marks Gallery, New York

83 *Crepuscule.* 1954. Tempera, $12^{1}/_{4} \times 12''$. Signed and dated lower right. Collection Marian Willard Johnson, New York

84 *The Shroud of Christ.* 1954. Tempera on paper, $10^{3}/_{4} \times 7^{1}/_{4}''$. Signed and dated lower right. Owned by the artist

85 *Voyagers III.* 1954. Tempera on paper, $17^{3}/_{4} \times 11^{7}/_{8}''$. Signed and dated lower right. Collection Governor Nelson A. Rockefeller, New York

86 *Night.* 1954. Tempera on paper, $17^{1}/_{4} \times 12''$. Signed and dated lower right. Collection Marian Willard Johnson, New York

*87 *The Avenue.* 1954. Tempera and watercolor on composition board, $40 \times 30^{1}/_{4}''$. Signed and dated lower right. Norton Gallery and School of Art, West Palm Beach, Florida. Ill. p. 74

88 *Forest Cathedral.* 1955. Tempera on paper, $20^{1}/_{2} \times 15''$. Signed and dated lower right. Galerie Beyeler, Basel

89 *Fountains of Europe.* 1955. Tempera and watercolor, $17^{1}/_{8} \times 22^{3}/_{8}''$. Signed and dated lower right. Museum of Fine Arts, Boston

90 *Moon.* 1955. Tempera on composition board. $29^{3}/_{4} \times 39^{1}/_{2}''$. Signed and dated lower right. Collection Mr. and Mrs. Andrew E. Norman, Palisades, New York

91 *Flight.* 1955. Ink on paper, $17^{3}/_{4} \times 11^{7}/_{8}''$. Signed and dated lower right. Otto Seligman Gallery, Seattle

92 *White Journey.* 1956. Tempera on paper, $44^{3}/_{4} \times 35^{1}/_{4}''$. Signed and dated lower right. Galerie Beyeler, Basel

93 *Pacific Circle.* 1956. Tempera, $44 \times 34^{3}/_{4}''$. Signed and dated lower right. Willard Gallery, New York

94 *Battle of the Lights.* 1956. Tempera on paper, $43^{1}/_{2} \times 35''$. Signed and dated lower right. Collection Mr. and Mrs. Harry Lewis Winston, Birmingham, Michigan

95 *Plains Ceremonial.* 1956. Tempera on cardboard, $24^{3}/_{8} \times 36^{1}/_{8}''$. Signed and dated lower left. The Joseph H. Hirshhorn Foundation, Inc.

*96 *Above the Earth V.* 1956. Tempera, $18 \times 11^{3}/_{4}''$. Signed and dated lower left. Collection Mr. and Mrs. Richard Lippold, Locust Valley, New York. Ill. p. 77

97 *Above the Earth.* 1957. Tempera, $24 \times 17^{1}/_{2}''$. Signed and dated lower right. Collection G. David Thompson, Pittsburgh

98 *Space Continuum.* 1957. Tempera on composition board, $40 \times 30''$. Signed and dated lower right. The Baltimore Museum of Art. Harry A. Bernstein Memorial Collection

99 *October.* 1957. Tempera on paper, $28^{1}/_{4} \times 44^{1}/_{4}''$. Signed and dated lower right. Galerie Beyeler, Basel

100 *Calligraphy in White*. 1957. Tempera on paper, 35×23¼″. Signed and dated lower right. Collection Otto D. Seligman, Seattle

101 *New York Night*. 1957. Tempera on paper, 36¼×24⅜″. Signed and dated lower right. Collection Mr. and Mrs. Hans Arnhold, New York

*102 *Dragonade*. 1957. Sumi (ink) on paper, 24⅜×34⅛″. Signed and dated lower right. Milwaukee Art Center. Gift of Mrs. Edward R. Wehr. Ill. p. 78

103 *Robber Barons*. 1957. Sumi (ink) on paper, 24×34″. Signed and dated lower right. Collection Mr. and Mrs. Solomon B. Smith, Lake Forest, Illinois

104 *Space Ritual VII*. 1957. Sumi (ink) on paper, 39×26¾″. Signed and dated lower left. Willard Gallery, New York

*105 *Space Ritual XIII*. 1957. Sumi (ink) on paper, 50⅜×26¼″. Signed and dated lower left. Willard Gallery, New York. Ill. p. 79

106 *Composition No. I*. 1957. Sumi (ink) on paper, 24×38½″. Signed and dated lower right. Collection G. David Thompson, Pittsburgh

107 *Long Island Spring*. 1957. Sumi (ink) on paper, 24×19½″. Signed and dated lower right. Collection Marian Willard Johnson, New York

108 *Circle and Thrusts*. 1957. Sumi (ink) on paper, 24×38¾″. Signed and dated lower right. Owned by the artist

109 *Head*. 1957. Sumi (ink) on paper, 21×14¾″. Signed and dated lower right. Collection Mr. and Mrs. C. Ron Johnsone, Seattle

110 *In the Grass*. 1958. Tempera on paper, 18⅛×16⅛″. Signed and dated lower right. Willard Gallery, New York

111 *Threading White*. 1958. Tempera on paper, 24×19½″. Signed and dated lower right. Collection Mr. and Mrs. Harold Diamond, New York

112 *Night Flight*. 1958. Tempera on paper, 10½×7½″. Signed and dated lower right. Galerie Beyeler, Basel

113 *Prophetic Light*. 1958. Tempera, 60¼×34¾″. Signed and dated lower left. Collection Marian Willard Johnson, New York

*114 *Medieval Landscape*. 1958. Tempera on paper, 17×34⅝″. Signed and dated lower right. Collection N. Richard Miller, New York. Ill. p. 73

*115 *Jeweled Jungle*. 1958. Tempera and ink on cardboard, 9¼×13¾″. Signed and dated lower right. Willard Gallery, New York. Ill. p. 80

*116 *World* (1959). Tempera, 11¾″ diameter. Collection Marian Willard Johnson, New York. Ill. p. 8

*117 *Space Rose*. 1959. Tempera on paper, 15¾×11¾″. Signed and dated lower right. Galerie Jeanne Bucher, Paris. Ill. p. 82

118 *Space Lines*. 1959. Tempera on paper, 9⅞×7⅞″. Signed and dated lower right. Collection Rudolph Indlekofer, Basel

119 Untitled. 1959. Tempera on paper, 35×23⅝″. Signed and dated lower right. Collection Mr. and Mrs. Arthur L. Dahl, Pebble Beach, California

120 *Early Thaw*. 1959. Tempera on paper, 6⅛×8⅞″. Signed and dated lower right. Willard Gallery, New York

*121 *Plane of Poverty*. 1960. Oil on canvas, 76¼×45½″. Signed and dated lower right. Collection Mr. and Mrs. Ira Haupt, Asbury Park, New Jersey. (Exhibited in New York only). Ill. p. 81

122 Untitled. 1960. Oil on canvas, 78×65″. Signed and dated lower left. Carnegie Institute, Pittsburgh. Patrons Art Fund

123 *Void I*. 1960. Tempera on paper, 6¾×4¾″. Signed and dated lower right. Willard Gallery, New York

*124 *Void II*. 1960. Tempera on paper, 6¾×4⅞″. Signed and dated lower right. Willard Gallery, New York. Ill. p. 2

125 *Page from the Universal*. 1960. Tempera on paper, 18⅞×24½″. Signed and dated lower right. Collection Mr. and Mrs. Arthur G. Barnett, Seattle

*126 *Homage to Rameau*. 1960. Tempera on black paper, 6¾×8″. Signed and dated lower right. Willard Gallery, New York. Ill. p. 52

127 *Lovers of Light*. 1960. Tempera on paper, 4¾×6¾″. Signed and dated lower right. Willard Gallery, New York

128 *Space Wall*. 1960. Tempera on paper, 4½×4¾″. Signed and dated lower right. Willard Gallery, New York

129 *Winter I*. 1960. Tempera and glue, 10½×6″. Otto Seligman Gallery, Seattle

130 *The Little Sun*. 1960. Tempera on paper, 3⅜×3½″. Signed and dated lower right. Owned by the artist

131 *Other World I*. 1961. Tempera and varnish on paper, 8½×6¾″. Signed and dated lower right. Willard Gallery, New York

132 *Other World III*. 1961. Tempera and varnish on paper, 7¼×16⅜″. Signed and dated lower right. Willard Gallery, New York

133 Untitled. 1961. Tempera and sand on paper, 4¾×6¾″. Signed and dated lower right. Willard Gallery, New York

134 *After the Imprint*. 1961. Tempera, 39¼×27¼″. Signed and dated lower right. The Phillips Collection, Washington. (Exhibited in New York only)

*135 *Signature I*. 1961. Tempera and glue on paper, 8½×11⅝″. Signed and dated lower right. Owned by the artist. Ill. (detail) on cover